"*How to Talk to Your Kids about School Violence* is a hands-on, easy-to-read, easy-to-follow guide that helps you with a step-by-step approach to talking to your kids. I found myself nodding in agreement with the turn of each page."　　—Dawn Anna, *mother of four including slain Columbine student Lauren Townsend*

*　*　*

"After the family, the school is the most crucial environment for learning values, including self-control and nonviolence. Dr. Druck's book will be a precious instrument in the hands of parents who are concerned about the future of their children."
—Dr. Abdelkader Abbadi, *Former Deputy-Director of the United Nations Security Council*

*　*　*

"It takes only one child to inflict violence on a school. This invaluable book offers practical ways for parents to talk to their children and encourages them to communicate with the schools."　　—Karen Degischer, *Principal, Santana H.S.*

"Dr. Druck's eminently practical, thoughtful and sensible book will jumpstart serious conversations within our families and neighborhoods. Dialogues that result will make a crucial contribution to the security and education concerns that now rightly dominate our national agenda."   —Alan Bersin, *Superintendent of San Diego City Schools former U.S. Atty., Southern District of CA*

* * *

"Ken Druck's guidebook provides a smart, strategic series of down-to-earth insights, practices and tools which will enable parents and students to better communicate and collaborate, so they can truly prevent school violence."
—Senator John Vasconcellos, *author of California's landmark 2002 legislation for preventing school violence*

* * *

"Rarely are parents given practical tools to help make their children and their schools safer. This book provides this vital information in a way that is easy, even fun, to read. If every parent read this book, our nation's schools and schoolchildren would be much safer."   —Daniel Gross, *co-founder, PAX—Real Solutions to Gun Violence*

DEDICATIONS

To Jenna and Stefie with all my heart
for the joy and privilege of being your father.
—K.D.

For Su and Anna—my two eternal lights.
—M.K.

Onomatopoeia, Inc.
Print and Audio Publishers Since 1975
49 West 27th Street, New York, NY 10001

Publisher's Cataloging-in-Publication
(Provided by Quality Books, Inc.)

Druck, Ken.
    How to talk to your kids about school violence / by
Ken Druck with Matthew Kaplowitz ; foreward by Ken
Blanchard ; illustrations by Arnie Levin. -- 1st ed.
    p. cm.
    Includes index.
    LCCN 2003109089
    ISBN 0-9722342-0-9

    1. School violence.   I. Kaplowitz, Matthew.
II. Title.

LB3013.3.D78 2003   371.7'82
                      QBI03-200544

Printed in the United States of America

1 2 3 4

Book design by Raymond Hooper Design
Website design by BabcockMedia.com

FOR MORE INFORMATION ABOUT
HOW TO TALK TO YOUR KIDS ABOUT SCHOOL VIOLENCE
Learning Materials, Audio Book Version and Author Speaking Engagements
(212) 213-9796
www.HowToTalkToYourKids.com

HOW TO TALK TO YOUR KIDS ABOUT SCHOOL VIOLENCE

BY **DR. KEN DRUCK**

WITH **MATTHEW KAPLOWITZ**

FOREWORD BY **DR. KEN BLANCHARD**

ILLUSTRATIONS BY **ARNIE LEVIN**

ONOMARK, NY

CONTENTS

FOREWORD

BY DR. KEN BLANCHARD

When I think about school violence, I am sad. Why? Because I know there are so many alternatives to dealing with conflict and unexpressed feelings other than violence. Unfortunately a lot of kids don't. It seems that "an eye for an eye" philosophy is alive and well among young people in schools. If someone does something to you, then you have the right to get even—and violence is often the result. And yet, as Gandhi once contended, "The problem with an eye for an eye is that eventually everyone in the world will be blind." We need to teach young people alternative philosophies. They need different role models.

People are always asking me, "Where can I look for role models?" My mission statement is to "be a loving teacher and example of simple truths that helps myself and others to awaken the presence of God in our lives." The reason I mention God is I think we need to lead our lives at a higher level and look for role models among spiritual leaders like Gandhi, Jesus, Buddha, Moses, and Mohammed, who believed and lived according to higher standards.

These spiritual leaders were enlightened enough to say, "Let's find a way to live . . . in peace." They encourage us to move from violence to caring about each other, from violence to living life at a higher level. They taught us to use the time we have here to make a positive difference in each other's lives. We can take away fear, we can take away violence, we can take away all of the negative things if we put our conscious energy at a higher level. Maybe we ought to put these spiritual leaders out front so their teachings can be a real part of our lives, help us behave differently, and set better role models for our kids.

Good parenting is about setting good examples. That involves how to treat other people in front of your kids. How you act when things don't go your way. We have to be positive role models for our children by showing them how to get along in life. We also need to talk with them. I have learned, from experience, that our children listen, even if they don't show it. One of my greatest thrills in life is to hear my son, Scott, saying things to his two young boys, Kurtis and Kyle, that I said to him as a boy.

Your kids are always watching you. They're watching you 24 hours a day. And you have to be a role model for them. You have to be someone who can show them there's a different way to deal with the world. That's why Ken Druck's book *How to Talk to Your Kids About School Violence,* is so important. It shows literally hundreds of ways you can make a difference in your kids' lives, and how they in turn can make a difference in other kids' lives.

I have long been an admirer of Ken Druck. Ken cares about people, he cares about kids and their families, and he wants to make a difference in our lives. His present ministry with kids started out of tragedy—the loss of his fabulous daughter, Jenna. As a result he created the Jenna Druck Foundation to help other families deal with the worst nightmare we all fear: losing a child. The Families Helping Families outreach program of the Jenna Druck Foundation is focused on what all of us can do to make the world a safer place for our kids and what our kids themselves can do to prevent tragedies in their schools.

Faith alone can't make the difference. We need practical, easy-to-understand strategies we can use right in our own homes. *How to Talk with Your Kids About School Violence* provides these strategies and the tools to implement them. We must do everything in our power to make the world safer for our children and grandchildren, beginning with educating ourselves. The future rests on it! God bless us all with peace.

San Diego, California
August 2002

INTRODUCTION

Being a parent has been the greatest challenge and the greatest privilege of my life. Life's most profound lessons have come from raising and being raised by two bright, independent daughters. Counseling families for the past twenty-six years has also taught me a lot about parenting. I've learned that the most important and positive impact we can have on our children is by talking—and *listening*—to them.

My daughter Jenna died young. She was only twenty-one. Since her death, I have devoted my life to saving kids' lives, and to helping the families of children who die. Our children all deserve to graduate from high school, go to college, get a job, start a family and live out their lives. And we deserve to be there, proudly watching as their lives unfold. No parent should have to endure the horror and pain of losing a child to violence. And no child should have to die at the hands of another. So what can we do to prevent violence?

There has never been a more important time to stand up and be counted as a parent. Our children are more vulnerable than ever. We must talk to them about school violence and how to prevent it. Starting in our own homes, we can make a difference. We can reduce the threat of violence that claims thousands of young lives each year in our country by educating our own children.

School violence is not only about dangerous, out-of-control kids on the "other side" of town. It is about all of our children. Our society. Our child's school. And us. We can't afford to distance ourselves from this problem. Dawn Anna, mother of Lauren, a eighteen-year-old student at Columbine High School, and Mary Gordon, mother of Randy, a fifteen-year-old student at Santana High School will tell you. School violence can and does happen. Not just to somebody else's child. To our children. And to *us*. And it's up to *us* to prevent it from happening again.

Making our child's world safer means many things: educating them about safety, making their schools safer, helping them develop peaceful ways of dealing with conflict and adversity, teaching them to manage their anger, and being good role models. If this seems a bit overwhelming, there's a reason.

Raising kids is no easy task. Neither is talking to them about their safety. You will have successes and you will make mistakes. The biggest mistake is to think we as parents *should* have all the answers, or that we *should* already know exactly how to talk to our children. We need help. Sometimes we need reminders that we're going to make mistakes, we're only human, and we're doing the best that we can. You will find these reminders, which we call "Reality Checks," in every chapter:

> **Reality Check** There's no such thing as a perfect parent. Never was. Never will be. So, go easy on yourself and your child. It takes time, patience, hard work, and courage to be a good parent. Progress can be slow. Give it your best shot today. Keep practicing. And you'll do even better tomorrow.

I wrote *How to Talk to Your Kids About School Violence* to show parents how to talk to their children about safety and be effective. In the coming chapters, you will find the most up-to-date information on violence prevention and safety practices, as well as practical guidelines for talking to your child, even when they don't want to listen. You'll learn to tune in to your child's world, teach them how to recognize and deal with a potentially violent situation, escape a dangerous situation, handle a bully, and report a threat. You will know exactly what to tell them to do if they see a gun in someone's backpack or at a friend's house. Overall, you'll learn how to talk to your child about staying safe.

You picked up this book because you are concerned about your children's safety. You cannot be there every second to protect them, or control everything that happens to them. But you can prepare them for the world they're going to encounter. By doing this, you make the world just that much safer for your child, and for us all.

CHAPTER 1

VERY 20 SECONDS IN THE U.S. A CHILD IS ARRESTED.—CDF ■ U.S. KIDS ARE 10 TIMES MORE LIKELY TO COMMIT

IURDER THAN COMPARABLY-AGED CANADIANS.—CDF ■ 160,000 KIDS MISS SCHOOL DAILY DUE TO FEAR OF ATTACK,

GETTING

EER INTIMIDATION, OR BULLYING.—NEA ■ HYPERACTIVITY AND ATTENTION DEFICITS HAVE INCREASED

STARTED

N TWO DECADES.—AMA ■ ADOLESCENT DEPRESSION HAS INCREASED 1000% IN 40 YEARS.—AMA ■ ADOLESCENT

UICIDE HAS INCREASED 400% IN 30 YEARS.—AAP ■ 73% OF 10-TO-18-YEAR-OLDS HIT SOMEONE DURING THE

EAR BECAUSE OF ANGER.—JIE ■ 24% OF HIGH SCHOOL STUDENTS SAY THEY TOOK A WEAPON TO SCHOOL AT LEAST

NCE IN PAST YEAR.—JIE ■ IN 10 YEARS JUVENILE THEFT HAS INCREASED 22%.—FBI[1] ■ ONE OUT OF 5 FIFTH-

RADERS HAS BEEN DRUNK; TWO-THIRDS OF EIGHTH GRADERS HAVE USED ALCOHOL.—AAP ■ ANTISOCIAL

EHAVIORS CAN BE STOPPED OR AT LEAST REDIRECTED INTO MORE ACCEPTABLE DIRECTIONS.—BORBA[1]

Violence is everywhere. On TV. In movies. In video games. In music. The childhood we wanted for our children did not have airplanes crashing into tall buildings, school shootings, anthrax in the mail, or terrorist alerts. In addition to invading our cities, towns, schools, and neighborhoods, violence has become commonplace in too many of our families.

Our nation changed after Columbine High School students and teachers were killed. Schools and communities dedicated themselves to improving safety and preventing violence in our young people. We began to confront the high degree of violence in our society and how it is adversely affecting our children.

Since the terrorist attacks of September 11, 2001, our concerns have intensified. The safety and sanctity of our nation were shattered—this time by an indiscriminate strain of murderous violence called terrorism. As we dig ourselves out of the emotional rubble and adjust to the realities of homeland security, *safety* is our number one concern.

How do we protect ourselves, our children, and our way of life?

We play a vital role in the lives of our children, many of whom are filled with fear, anxiety, confusion, and anger. We are just beginning to understand the full impact of the high school shootings and terrorist attacks on the young people of our nation. But this we do know: our children need us more than ever. Are we doing everything in our power to make their world safer? To really "be there" for them?

We'd all like to think our kids will come to us when they're in trouble . . . when they're angry, or afraid . . . when they're in danger . . . or when there are weapons in their school. But will they? Some of us are confident—our kids have open lines of communication with us. They come to us freely for help. Others feel painfully cut off from our children. No matter what your communication with your child is like, all of us are working on being better parents. And that's what counts.

BUILDING BRIDGES: THE FIRST 10 STEPS

Building a stronger relationship with your children begins with you. Your attitude. Your tone. Your commitment. Your knowledge. And your effectiveness as a communicator. Building bridges takes patience, and not being oversensitive or easily discouraged. As you begin reading this book, consider these ten small but positive steps:

1. **Connect with your child.** Become more a part of her world. Take more of an interest in her life. Be less critical and more friendly to her—like a parent, not a "pal." Greet her in a positive way. Show her physical affection. Ask how she's doing. Give her compliments. Get to know her friends. Get to know her world, including music, video games, TV shows, books, movie stars and athletes she likes. Attend her school events or after-school activities whenever you can. Notice when she does something well, and tell her, "Great job!" When she doesn't succeed, pat her on the back and reassure her. Open your heart even wider to her. Open hearts make for open communication.

2. **Have regular heart-to-heart talks.** Nothing establishes confidence and trust between you and your child more than talking to each other from your hearts. This keeps the lines of communication open in good times and bad.

3. **Set realistic expectations.** Don't set yourself up for disappointment or failure by expecting too much too soon. Kids open up when they feel safe. This may take time, and patience.

4. **Involve your spouse, partner, a relative or friend.** As a parent, it helps to have someone you can vent to and bounce ideas off; someone who feels comfortable telling you you're doing a good job—or that you are getting off course. Always work together as a parenting "team," even if you and your child's other parent are no longer together.

5. **Clean house.** Clear your important relationships of anger, bitterness, or old grudges. This may mean apologizing, accepting an apology, or both. Some "emotional baggage" requires professional help, but in most cases, you'll just need to talk it out.

6. **It's OK not to have all the answers.** We won't always have the right thing to say at the right moment. Give yourself time to figure all this out. Be willing to listen and learn something new each step of the way.

7. **Open the safety conversation.** Many parents have "the talk" with their kids about drugs and alcohol, and the one about sex. But we must also open the equally important conversation about safety and violence. Tell your kids you love them and are committed to their happiness and well-being. Explain that you have been thinking a lot about their safety and reading this book about how to prevent violence. Then, discuss what you're learning.

8. **Know that immediate danger requires immediate action.** If you discover your child is at risk and in immediate danger, act right away. Contact your child's school counselor or principal, a child therapist, or even the police for help.

9. **Face reality.** None of us wants to think that our child is capable of hurting anyone. Or being in trouble. Coming to terms with the "dark side" of our children's behavior is one of the toughest parts of being a parent. We'd sometimes rather be in denial. The "Not my kid!" approach is dangerous. A call from the principal, police, neighbor, or parents of our child's friend should not be what it takes to make us admit there is a problem. By facing reality, we begin the process of solving underlying problems and prevent our child from getting into further trouble.

10. **Don't give up.** Just because you're trying a new approach doesn't mean your children will act differently overnight. There will be setbacks. They'll push your buttons. All kids do. Go one step at a time and don't give up no matter what.

"YEAH, WHATEVER . . .": GETTING PAST COMMUNICATION ROADBLOCKS

Getting through to our kids can be difficult. They can be extremely sensitive and defensive. Resistant. Downright stubborn. Building bridges often involves trying something new. How can you get past their communication roadblocks and other diversionary tactics? The trick is to keep your focus. Be patient. Most important, be smart. Don't let them change the subject, talk you out of it, prey upon your guilt, or sucker you into an argument. Take no detours. Accept no excuses. Better listening, being direct in bringing up tough issues, setting firm limits, and taking more time face-to-face will help you get through to your child.

When you are ready to tackle thorny subjects like their friends, their safety, or what's going on in school and you hit a roadblock, here are some "smart responses":

When your kids say:	YOU should say:
"What did I do now?"	"You haven't done anything wrong, you aren't in trouble. I just want to ask you some questions about school."
"You treat me like a child! I'm xx years old now." Or, "I've gotten this far. Why should we talk now?"	"That's why I want to talk to you. Because you *are* old enough and mature enough to have this discussion."
"This is so lame." Or, "This is ridiculous." Or, "I can't believe we have to talk about this."	"This isn't lame/ridiculous/stupid. This is about your safety."
"Don't you trust me?"	"Trust is not all or nothing. We trust more or less, depending on how the other person acts."
"None of my friends have to sit and talk about all this stuff."	"Your friends' parents might not discuss this, but we need to."

When your kids say:	**YOU should say:**
"We don't NEED to talk about anything!" Or, "Get over it. You're just being paranoid." Or, "You guys are crazy!"	"Look, I'm sorry if you don't like it, but there are some things we need to discuss. If now isn't convenient, then fine, but we *are* going to talk about this."
"Why can't you ever just leave me alone!" Or, "I'm busy!"	"This is important. When is a good time to talk?"

Reality Check Just because you want to talk to your kids doesn't mean they're ready. Don't be surprised if you try to jump into a conversation and you run head on into resistance. If you're having a hard time bringing some of these things up, hang in there. Most parents go through this. Continue to practice the "What you should say" responses in your own words. And reread "Building Bridges: The First Ten Steps" until you've memorized it!

10 MORE TIPS FOR GETTING STARTED

1. **Pick a time and place you won't be interrupted.**
   The family room has always worked for me. A booth at the local pizza joint may be even better.

2. **Open with something light,** like a funny story, not doom and gloom.

3. **Ask them to talk with you.** Tell them, "It's very important to me to discuss these things. Please just try it." Express each concern giving real-life examples.

4. **Ask what they think.** Listen, don't criticize or give advice.

5. **Tell them it's OK to differ with you,** but set clear limits and boundaries for discussions. (See Chapter 4.)

6. **Be supportive as they begin to open up.** For example, you might tell them that it's natural to feel angry, scared, or vengeful.

7. **Suggest ground rules.** If things go a little sideways during your talk, mutually agree: no shouting, no interrupting, no swearing, or walking out of the room. And establish that you'll always respect each other's point of view.

8. **Monitor your voice.** If you hear yourself sounding too harsh or critical, bring it down a notch. A toned-down "Why did you do *that*?" helps maintain calm in rough waters; a warm voice conveys sincerity, and so on.

9. **Keep it short and simple.** Build on each small success.

10. **End on a positive note.** Thank your child for talking to you.

CONVERSATION STOPPERS

If you have a knack for putting your foot into your mouth, you'll need to watch your words with your child. Here are seven common mistakes that bring parent-child conversations to a screeching halt:

1. Blanket reassurances like:

- "You'll be fine!" "You'll get over it!"

- "That's life."

- "You can handle it! You're tough."

2. Trying to talk your child out of how she's feeling, telling her she's wrong to feel angry, hurt, etc.

3. Resorting to "power" tactics and punishment. Making demands, giving orders followed by a "Because I said so!"

4. Rushing and hurrying your child:

- "Get to the point!

- "I don't have all day!"

5. Dismissing your child's concerns:

- "What's the big deal? There's nothing to get upset about."

- "Don't worry about it. Everyone goes through this."

- "Just leave it alone. Things will work out. This is nothing."

- "When I was your age, things were much tougher." (Not!)

- "Everybody gets called names . . . it's not like he hit you."

6. Using shame, accusing, or comparing your child:

- "You're acting like a child."

- "You don't care about anybody but yourself."

- "Why can't you be more like your sister or your friend so-and-so?"

7. Punishing harshly when your child confesses to doing something wrong.

Teaching your kids what they need to know about safety starts with you. It may be rough going at first. Tackling touchy subjects and changing long-established family patterns is no easy matter. Yet we are willing to do all this because our children's safety is at risk. We cannot leave it to others. *How to Talk to Your Kids about School Violence* provides guidelines, but you must adapt them to your child. Each child is different. And children change as they get older. Find out what works with your child and start doing it. Being a good role model comes next.

Reality Check "It takes a village to raise a child." We can't do it alone. Throughout this book I may suggest that you "seek professional help" or "consult an expert." Family and school counselors, child psychologists, clergy, and social workers are trained to help our kids and families. In addition, parent-effectiveness coaches, anger management specialists, substance abuse counselors, and your own local police department's school safety program counselors can be valuable resources. Never be shy when it comes to asking for help. Affordable—or free—professional services are available to everyone.

CHAPTER **2**

WITNESS ABUSE AT HOME. 79% OF THOSE CHILDREN TURN TO VIOLENT BEHAVIOR.—*YWCA*[1] ■ A FREQUENTLY AGGRES-

IVE CHILD OR ADOLESCENT IS VERY LIKELY TO GROW UP TO BE A HIGHLY AGGRESSIVE ADULT, AND MORE LIKELY TO

BEING A

OMMIT VIOLENT CRIMES, DRUNK DRIVING, CHILD AND SPOUSE ABUSE.—*CRA* ■ ONE LONG-TERM STUDY SHOWED

ROLE

SIGNIFICANT RELATIONSHIP BETWEEN THE LEVEL OF VIOLENCE AT 8 YEARS OF AGE AND ANTISOCIAL ACTS 22 YEARS

MODEL

ATER.—*CRA* ■ MORE THAN HALF OF ALL PARTICIPANTS IN THE NATIONAL YOUTH SURVEY WITH RECORDS OF VIOLENT

EHAVIOR BEGAN TO ENGAGE IN SUCH BEHAVIOR BETWEEN THE AGES OF 14 AND 17.—*NIH* ■ VIOLENT YOUTHS WITH VIO-

ENT PARENTS ARE FAR MORE LIKELY TO HAVE MODELED THEIR BEHAVIOR ON THEIR PARENTS' BEHAVIOR THAN SIMPLY

O HAVE INHERITED IT FROM THEM.—*USSG*[1] ■ STUDIES SHOW THAT PARENT TRAINING CAN LEAD TO CLEAR IMPROVE-

MENTS IN CHILDREN'S ANTISOCIAL BEHAVIOR, AGGRESSION, AND FAMILY MANAGEMENT PRACTICES.—*USSG*[2]

Our children are watching us. They see and hear everything. They watch us as we yell at the driver who cuts us off in traffic. And they watch us at our best as we lend a hand to a stranger. More than anywhere else, our children are watching us right here at home. They see us handle family disputes about whose television show gets picked, who broke the garage window, and when bedtime is on school nights. They also watch to see whether Mom and Dad kiss and make up after a fight.

You are the role model for your children. And learning to deal with conflict begins at home. Giving your children the right tools to constructively handle their emotions and the differences they'll encounter with others is the first step in violence prevention.

Reality Check Let's face it, as much as we aspire to be great role models and "walk the talk" there will be times we fall short. Don't be too hard on yourself if you find yourself asking your child to do as you say, not as you do. We're all trying our best to become better people and better parents. Having integrity doesn't mean you're perfect, it means you work hard to close the gap between your words and deeds.

STOCKING YOUR CHILD'S TOOLBOX

We all use coping and communication "tools" to deal with daily life— some of us better than others. These tools become our means to express anger, deal with fear, handle setbacks, negotiate differences, and build trust. They help us take on life. As a parent, it's your job to put good tools in your child's toolbox.

Through your example, your children learn how to get along with others. You *show* your children how to be respectful—not hostile. By watching you, they learn to deal with their emotions in a healthy and safe manner. Family disagreements become opportunities for your kids to see conflict handled constructively.

Here are some behaviors we want our children to learn by our example:

SHOW COMPASSION AND RESPECT

Do our children see us as empathic and sensitive, not only to each other at home but to *all* people, whether or not they're like us? Or do people who are different bother us so much that we exclude and ridicule them, making them feel lesser so we feel greater? Do our children hear us gossiping, judging, or trashing others behind their backs?

We want to be adults who show respect and compassion for all people. In my family, our children's views toward the homeless changed drastically when we began taking them with us to help serve meals at shelters. Compassion and respect will help children develop their natural capacity for empathy and understanding.

PERFORM ACTS OF KINDNESS

Pats on the back. An encouraging word. Cushioning a nasty blow. Sharing someone's loss. Don't underestimate the message you're sending to your children when you act kindly. My daughter Stefie recently recalled an incident from ten years ago that has stayed with her. After a soccer game in which her best friend had allowed the deciding goal, I went up to her friend and said, "Don't be so hard on yourself. You played a great game." Stefie told me, "Dad, I loved what you said to Jessica." Simple deeds like this set an example for a lifetime.

The Cycle of Kindness begins with one person showing compassion for another. That person reaches out to another with an act of kindness or courtesy.

That kindness or courtesy spreads as it is passed on to another person, and another, and another. Thus perpetuating the cycle of kindness.

The same cycle exists for hurt, anger, and even hatred. These emotions can be transferred from one person to another in a matter of moments.

And so, we are left with the choice: to perpetuate hatred or kindness. The choice is ours to make. The example is ours to set.

DEVELOP STRENGTH OF CHARACTER

Character is an interesting concept. It's more about inner calm, values, and confidence than flexing muscles. It's easy for our kids to confuse real strength of character with fake or "pseudo-strength." Pseudo-strength frequently comes dressed in the costumes of larger-than-life action heroes—like Rambo and the Terminator. These "heroes" resolve differences in only one way: using force.

People who possess character strength—real strength—have lots of tools for resolving differences. Their approach doesn't use power *over* another individual. They *share* power. Sharing power *with* others allows people to be different yet work toward a common goal. Sharing *power* rarely results in violence.

Character strength means teaching our children the virtues of honesty, integrity, self-discipline, dependability, loyalty, pride, and how to get along with others. It equips them with the communication tools and confidence to resolve differences nonviolently, to build bridges rather than burn them, to diffuse dangerous situations, and to be peacemakers. Resisting the use of force is a sign of strength, not of weakness.

CONTROL YOUR OWN ANGER

As the parent and primary role model, you want to make sure your anger is under control.

1. **Check your boiling point.** Your boss treats you unfairly. Your spouse keeps you waiting . . . and waiting. The umpire makes a bad call and your child is unfairly called, "Out!" Triggers for anger are everywhere. How do you react?

   - Do you yell, scream, or allow incidents like these to escalate into loud arguments or even violence?

   - Can you take a deep breath, turn around, and walk away from a potentially dangerous situation?

   - Do you retreat from conflict, or resort to indirect "passive-aggressive paybacks" like going behind somebody's back?

   - Can you turn a negative into a positive so that everyone walks away respecting each other's differences?

2. Bring down your boiling point. If you find yourself getting into constant arguments, if people are afraid of your explosiveness, or you often feel regret about how you "lost it," it's time to bring down your boiling point. Uncontrolled anger and harsh criticism send the wrong message to our children. They learn it's OK for *them* to be this way. Decide what anger-control techniques work for you and use them as often as necessary. It can be as simple as counting to ten, breathing deeply, taking a walk, splashing water on your face, saying a prayer, or simply telling yourself, "Do not react!" The object is to put a *thought* between your impulse and your action. And if you need help controlling your anger, consult an expert in anger management.

3. Ease up on yourself. We often become angry with ourselves because we've made a mistake or failed in our own eyes. Lighten up when things don't go your way. Accept that we all make mistakes. Self-forgiveness and patience are also valuable virtues to teach your child.

Reality Check Much as you try, sometimes you'll "lose it" and your child will storm off to his room. Wait until things cool down. Apologize to your child and ask him to cut you some slack. Chances are, he will. This paves the way to forgiving honest mistakes and acknowledging that we're all human.

LET YOUR KIDS SEE YOU COPE

Everyday upsets, more severe problems, and even serious crises all require good coping skills. Here's an effective three-step process:

1. **Slow down.** Take a few moments to breathe and gain control over your impulse to fight or take flight.

2. **Think.** Consider smart options. Safety is your main objective.

3. **React constructively.** Keep your cool and react in a way that fits the situation, not your emotions at that moment.

Some problems take time to resolve. Be patient and flexible. Don't fall into the trap of trying to do it all at once.

RELAX NATURALLY

Our children need positive examples of how to let go of frustration and stress. They need to see how we care for and replenish ourselves every day, how we create balance. We all need healthy ways of decompressing from a long day's work. Alcohol or drugs, food, television, video games, or obsessive Web surfing are not effective ways of reducing stress. Let your child see you engage in stress-reducing activities such as these:

- An exercise program—a fitness or stress-reduction class, a gym workout, doing yoga, jogging, walking the treadmill

- Household activities—gardening, working in the yard or house

- Outdoor activities—sports, bicycling, even after-dinner walks

- Quiet time—prayer, meditation, reading

- 15 minutes of "downtime" in the middle of the day

- Relaxation and rejuvenation pursuits such as music or a hobby

- Casual, easygoing conversation among friends

- Eating a balanced diet

- Getting a full night's sleep

LIGHTEN UP AND HAVE FUN

Each one of us has a playful side. When kids see only the hardworking, serious side of their parents, they miss out on a lot of fun. Laughter gives life balance and perspective. Children learn, through us, how healing "playful" fun and laughter can be. Let your children see you using humor and fun appropriately, never to hurt anyone.

A lighthearted approach can break down walls and tensions. For example, if your daughter lashes out at you, a lighthearted response like "I guess I do sound like a bit of a dork" can bring down the room temperature. Our family dog, Rascal, had a knack for sensing family tensions and would drop perfectly timed doggie stink bombs in the middle of a heated family argument.

TAKE RESPONSIBILITY FOR YOUR MISTAKES

How many of our children have seen us make a mistake and admit it? Or do we blame someone else? Sometimes the greatest teaching occurs in admitting to your children that you've made a mistake. Taking responsibility is a powerful tool for diffusing potentially violent situations. We can learn from our mistakes, and so can our children. It takes a "big man" or woman to admit they're wrong.

Try this: After admitting a mistake involving another person, apologize with your child present. Let your child see that apologizing reestablishes trust and good faith. Your apology says to your child that nobody is above making mistakes, that we're all accountable. And, perhaps most important, it vividly demonstrates one way to make amends and begin straightening things out.

Reality Check Everyone needs time out, even parents. When a conversation is moving so fast that you are all getting frustrated, or reach a stalemate, call a time-out. Get off the topic and share a snack with your child, take a few minutes by yourself to gather your thoughts, or ask for a rain check. Cool off! Come back refreshed.

GIVE SECOND CHANCES

Everyone makes mistakes. Getting along with others means forgiving others when they make mistakes—and letting things go. For example, ten years have passed since Uncle Al didn't invite you to his daughter's wedding. Al has mellowed with age and you've even grown to like him. Now your daughter is getting married. Is it time for payback or is it time to let bygones be bygones, bury the hatchet, and send Al an invitation?

Think of it this way:

- Holding a grudge is a lot of work. It takes a lot of energy to stay angry at someone, and it's a relief to finally let the anger go.

- Forgiving someone doesn't necessarily mean you're OK with what the other person did. It just means you're willing to let it go—and let the other person off the hook.

- Talk with your child about the many types of forgiveness, which can range from a good faith gesture of accepting a simple apology to a heart-to-heart talk about what hurt you, what hurt the other person, and suggestions for ways you can both change your behavior in the future.

- Forgiving someone takes time. Even when you're willing to forgive someone, hurt feelings take time to untangle and get over.

"FIGHT PEACEFULLY"

As a role model, how you approach disputes is at least as important as the result. To "fight peacefully" means talking to others with respect, whether or not we get our way. "Win-win" disagreements usually resolve rather than escalate conflicts.

Say your daughter is caught cheating but swears she's innocent. How do you react when you're sitting in the principal's office with your daughter and her teacher? Automatically taking your daughter's side may make matters worse. Calmly walking into the room with an open mind demonstrates your willingness to learn the facts and resolve the conflict.

What if, despite your daughter's defense, the school determines she was cheating? You again will have to be a role model, teaching that living with or calmly protesting the decisions of other people even when we disagree with them is a sign of character strength, not weakness. Our children face situations that are not fair. Sometimes it's important that they stand up for themselves. Other times they have to learn the difficult lesson that many battles are best left unfought. This is a crucial part of growing up.

We have to teach our children to stand up for themselves and for what they believe in—and to do it with self-control and with respect. We also need to show them when it's best to turn away, when to call for help, how to communicate when feeling upset, how to argue peacefully, and when not to fight at all.

HANDLE FAMILY CONFLICTS CONSTRUCTIVELY

All families fight. These fights are a training ground for our children. What do our children learn and how do they benefit when our family deals with upsets constructively? They learn that:

- Family members can be angry, disagree, AND be respectful. Families must eliminate the good or bad guy. Instead, we are people whose feelings can get hurt and who need to be understood.

- You issue the first apology: "I'm sorry. I was thinking only of myself." As parents we open the door to "family talk" in which everyone says how they feel and works toward a positive solution.

- You are a mediator: "Everyone is upset. Let's talk about what happened and how we hurt each other's feelings." This can sharpen our children's communication skills and build their confidence.

- All parties should talk it out before things reach the boiling point. New understandings and agreements are forged and the air is cleared. Children learn that anger is a healthy emotion. Angry feelings need not be hidden, denied, repressed, or couched as something else.

- Differences get worked out. Family members forgive and make up.

- Not all anger is OK. Out-of-control anger is not helpful or healthy.

PICK YOUR BATTLES

When we choose a "battle," when we choose to stand up for what's right, we're telling our child when to do the same—when to become involved without putting their own safety at risk. But this is not always possible. In rare instances we have to trade off our own safety to protect others. In the aftermath of the terrorist attacks of September 11, 2001, we saw this kind of heroism in firefighters, police, and the military, who put other people's lives ahead of their own.

But the "battles" we encounter every day are much simpler. Most of us are not trained professionals. We must rely on our good judgment in deciding which battles to fight, when to call for help, and when to walk away. It is said that "fools rush in . . . ." Show your children how to bring a sense of calm to any potentially violent situation. The best way to win a battle is not to allow it to turn into a war. Each dangerous situation you encounter as a parent needs to be handled differently. While clear guidelines are not always evident, there are some do's and don'ts to consider:

Don't get involved when:	**Do get involved when:**
The situation is highly dangerous and can better be handled by professionals.	You can prevent a bad situation from getting worse.
Weapons are involved and there's nothing you can do.	Your conscience tells you it's the right thing to do.
The situation requires a police response.	Someone is being seriously threatened and you are the only help available.
You have no idea what you are doing, and rushing in blindly could escalate the situation.	You have a plan that can lead to a positive outcome.
Someone is pressuring you to be a hero.	You have training that can help the immediate situation.

Be a good example. Put safety first and show your children how to meet a crisis head-on. Give them all the tools they need to defend themselves without resorting to violence. Teach them how, when, and where to call for help.

DISCUSS DISCRIMINATION AND HATRED

It's impossible to shield our children from the discrimination and hatred they are occasionally going to be exposed to on the street, in school, on television, in movies, or in music. Parents are too often unaware of how we unknowingly perpetuate dangerous attitudes and stereotypes. Do you talk openly about discrimination? Are you providing a model for all of "God's children" getting along, working out your differences? Show your kids the fine line between some forms of humor and hatred. Let your child know that destructive ethnic or sexist "jokes" can perpetuate negative stereotypes. Humor can hurt when it's tied to sarcasm, teasing, taunting, or making light of a serious situation.

After the terrorist attacks of 9/11, some of our differences melted away. We became more mindful of the threat posed by people who are driven to violence by hatred. The mass murder of innocent Americans unified us, and we realized that we are all just Americans, not "hyphenated" Americans.

BROADEN THEIR WORLD

It's important to realize that the friends we have, the company we keep, the places we take our children, and the different ethnic groups we expose them to broaden their world and bring others closer to them. When children are distanced from other kinds of people—and so many of our neighborhoods are still racially segregated—it makes it easier to perpetuate judgments, believe in stereotypes, and even, in some cases, justify violence against others.

CONNECT TO YOUR COMMUNITY

Our children need to know we care about what happens in our community. Let your child know that you vote, participate on juries, volunteer, support the PTA and speak out for what you believe in. This also goes for caring what happens in their school. Our kids learn to make a difference when they see us making a difference by participating in community affairs and activities.

It's important to involve ourselves in our community, even if it's only once a year. Cleaning a park or beach, rolling up our sleeves after a natural disaster, giving blood regularly, or painting an elderly person's home are ways to do this. What our children see us doing today, at home and out in the community, is what they will be doing tomorrow. Children who have had role models for constructive involvement in their communities often turn out to be role models for their siblings and friends.

History's great peacemaker Mahatma Gandhi said, "Be the change you want in the world." I adapt that to, "Be the change you want in your children." Show them the many alternatives to violence. Give them the tools. Leave them a legacy of peace.

CHAPTER **3**

S, AND PARENTAL MONITORING ARE PROTECTIVE FACTORS AGAINST RISK FACTORS FOR VIOLENCE.—*USSG*[1]

OF HIGH SCHOOL PUPILS LIED TO THEIR PARENTS IN THE PAST YEAR; MORE THAN ONE IN FOUR SAID THEY

LISTENING

LD LIE TO GET A JOB.—*US N&WR* ■ IN 1997, 3.5% OF HIGH SCHOOL STUDENTS NATIONWIDE WERE TREATED BY

AND

OCTOR OR A NURSE FOR INJURIES SUSTAINED IN A FIGHT.—*US DOE*[1] ■ YOUTHS WHO COMMIT THE MOST

TALKING

OUS VIOLENT ACTS, AND WHO CONTINUE THEIR VIOLENT BEHAVIOR BEYOND ADOLESCENCE, BEGIN DURING

DHOOD.—*USSG*[3] ■ POOR PARENT-CHILD RELATIONS, HARSH, LAX, OR INCONSISTENT DISCIPLINE, ABUSIVE

NEGLECTFUL PARENTS, POOR SUPERVISION AND MONITORING, AND LOW PARENTAL INVOLVEMENT ARE

SIDERED RISK FACTORS FOR VIOLENCE.—*USSG*[1] ■ SINCE 1969, HIGH SCHOOL PUPILS' TEST CHEATING

EASED FROM 34% TO 68%.—*US N&WR* ■ VIOLENCE IS LEARNED AND THEREFORE IS PREVENTABLE.—*BORB/*

Think back to your own youth . . . . Was the door open for you to go to your parents with your problems? Now ask yourself: When was the last time your child came to you asking for help?

"Being there" for our kids is the cornerstone of good parenting. Our willingness to simply talk and listen to our children, day in and day out, means more than expensive birthday presents or trips to Disneyland. Kids who have an open-door relationship with their parents are very fortunate. In addition to receiving lots of tender loving care, they're more likely to signal when they're in trouble and ask for help.

LISTEN FIRST

Good listening is the best tool for opening the lines of communication with your child—and keeping them open. Listening opens us to the world of our children's emotions, including their innermost fears and worries. Our children come to us with their problems and questions only when they feel "safe." Safety comes with knowing from experience that telling the truth results in help, not punishment.

Listening also allows our children to unburden themselves. They feel cared about and understood. Usually, afterward, they feel better. Being able to vent and have somebody listen—nothing more—allows children to solve most of their own problems. Good listening is woven into every strategy in this book. (*See Online Resource Directory, "Characteristics of a Good Listener".*)

But good listening requires restraint. Before we jump in, we need to train ourselves to listen first. We also need to learn how to ask the right questions. Great teachers, philosophers, clergy, lawyers, therapists, and hairdressers have known this for centuries. How do these masters of communication do it?

HOW TO USE OPEN-ENDED QUESTIONS

Once you've moved beyond the "yeah, whatever" stage and your child is beginning to trust you with what's on her mind, you've arrived at the next step—expanding the conversation. This is best done by using open-ended questions. Open-ended questions move us beyond "How's school? Fine" conversations to meaningful discussions.

By asking a good, open-ended question, you open the door for your child to tell you what's really on her mind. But "the door" will not open automatically, or all at once. Getting your child to open up, winning her trust, is a gradual process.

How do open-ended questions work? They give your child room to respond however he wishes. Children don't feel pressured to come up with the right answer. Open-ended questions are safe. They invite your child into a conversation in which it's OK to say how he really is. They reassure your child that it's OK to talk to you about real stuff. Some examples of open-ended questions that lead to open-ended discussions are:

- "What do you mean? Please explain."

- "What was it like for you when that happened?"

- "How has [this incident] made you feel different?"

- "How do your friends feel about this?"

- "Have you tried anything that made the situation better? Or worse?"

- "What do you think you should do next? What are your options?"

- "Is there anything I can do to help?"

- "Would you please tell me more about that?"

Be patient. Answers will not come immediately. We can't make our child, or anybody else, talk if he doesn't want to—but we can ask good, inviting questions and be a good listener.

TALKING: WHAT TO SAY

Once your child starts to talk, you'll want to draw him out. And listen. If you speak at all, it's only to encourage him to keep talking. Kids tend to be more interested in what you have to say if they feel you're interested in what they have to say. As the conversation progresses, you'll have a chance to chime in with your own thoughts.

Here are some tips for successful conversations with your children.

DON'T:

DO:

Don't send negative nonverbal signals such as disapproving looks, sighs, etc.

Give positive nods, smiles, and words of encouragement.

Don't ask leading questions that are really accusations.

Ask his opinion before asking if he'd like to hear yours.

Don't overreact, interrupt, or give unsolicited advice.

Commend him when he's handled a situation well.

Don't ridicule him, call him stupid or compare him to others.

Keep your feedback positive. Treat your child with respect, always.

Don't take over the conversation. *Really* listen.

Wait for the right time to express your view/opinion. If not in this conversation, next time.

Don't dismiss her concerns. Something that seems trivial to you can be a big deal to her.

Tell her you're trying to understand, but you need her help. Ask her to try explaining it in a different way.

Don't try to talk her out of how she is feeling.

Ask her if there are things you are saying that are making it harder for her to communicate.

Don't bring up things he previously confided or throw the past in his face.

Respect confidences and help him look to the future for opportunities to do better.

Don't push him. If a conversation hits the wall, back off. Never do anything that makes your child avoid talking to you.

Thank him for coming to you. Remember, successful discussions with our children happen one conversation at a time.

SHOW EMPATHY

Empathy is the ability to walk in someone else's shoes. We practice empathy in order to better understand the other person. Good parenting requires vast quantities of empathy. We need to feel what our children feel, to repeatedly put ourselves in their position, so we can know how the world appears from their perspective. When kids recognize that their feelings are being "heard" they are more willing to talk to us. They also learn how to be empathic themselves.

With practice, using empathic comments like these will come naturally:

- "You seem really upset about what happened."

- "I'm so sorry things didn't work out the way you wanted."

- "This must be very tough for you."

- "I can't imagine how frustrating this has been."

- "I can see how much this has really hurt you."

- "Your disappointment is so understandable."

- "I'm really sorry you have to go through this. It's terrible."

BITE YOUR TONGUE

Sometimes listening hurts. The things your kids say can hurt. Or make you angry. But remember: Never do anything that makes your child sorry she confided in you. This can be very hard for us as parents. The desire to snap back, or rush in with instant advice is almost irresistible.

Here's an example: Your daughter returns from her friend's house with purple hair. On her way home, schoolmates in a passing car yell profanities at her. She comes to you in tears, complaining about "those idiots." How do you react?

DON'T:

Don't blame her in the heat of the moment: "How did you expect people to react? Just look at you!"

Don't say or do something to put her on the defensive, such as, "Your sister never gets involved in this kind of trouble." Or, "Didn't I tell you not to do it?"

Don't join her in counterattacking the name-callers.

Don't use the incident to express your dislike of her hairstyle. Ask her if she wants to hear how you feel about her hair. If she says, "Yes," keep your comments positive. Share your concerns about the downside of purple hair and ask her whether it's worth it.

DO:

Tell her you are sorry this happened to her. "It's really terrible that other kids can be so mean."

Gently get her thoughts about what happened and why: "Please tell me what happened on your way home tonight."

Tell her you see how hurt and upset she is: "Something like this is never easy. Is there anything I can do?"

If possible, step back and let her make the final decision whether to change her hairstyle. She'll feel better about herself if it comes from her rather than from you, her parent.

Fighting the constant urge to tell our kids what to do, what not to do, and what we think is difficult. I have had to bite my tongue so many times the tip is frayed.

But listening must come first, before problem solving.

SEIZE THE MOMENT

Any time our kids volunteer information about themselves or their lives, it is a golden opportunity. Grab it, even if the time is inconvenient. I thought I could arrange sit-down talks with my daughters whenever I wanted. Good luck! Finding an opening to talk to your child can take place in a variety of settings and short conversations, so be on the lookout:

- During short trips in the car—you have a captive audience.

- In her room, making small talk over a snack.

- Upon hearing news about an incident at school.

- In discussion about a paper or artwork your child did for school.

- Upon hearing good or bad local, national, or international news.

- After watching a deeply inspiring movie, or a violent one.

- After reading aloud something that touches on the subject of violence in a newspaper, magazine, poem, or book.

- After attending a wedding, funeral, or special event.

- On a family outing or vacation when you have his undivided attention.

Remember, teenagers can be extremely sensitive. Even the slightest hint of criticism or judgment camouflaged in your questions can make them feel under attack and shut down the discussion. Go slowly, choose your words wisely, and listen attentively.

> **Reality Check** Some of our kids are so shut down that nothing we do or say gets a response. If you're not getting through, don't take this as a sign of failure. Instead, regroup—you may want to wait then try again. Or you may want your spouse, partner, or a friend to give it a try. Or you may need the help of an expert to get unstuck.

KEEP YOUR COOL

There are times when parents have to set limits and "lay down the law," and the sparks fly. Even these family firestorms can be opportunities to improve parent-child communication.

Listening and staying calm in the middle of a family firestorm tells your child:

- "I'm going to keep my cool even if you lose yours."

- "I'm listening. I respect and care about you."

- "I'm interested in what you have to say, but I can hear it a whole lot better when you say it with respect."

- "I hope you understand that the final decision is with me."

- "Even though we disagree, I'm confident we can come to a solution."

- "Even though we are angry, my love for you never changes."

Here's an example of keeping your cool: Your sixteen-year-old daughter is going out with her friends, and you tell her to "be home by ten." She's used to being out with her friends well past midnight on weekends, but there have been several gang shootings and rapes in your community and you don't want her on the streets. "Mom, I can't believe you!" she screams. "Why are you doing this to me? All my friend's parents let them stay out past ten. You are so lame! I hate you!"

Here are some do's and don'ts for handling situations like this:

DON'T:

Don't counterattack or pull rank. Screaming back, "Oh, yeah?? You're grounded for a week!!" only sets up a power struggle in which there will be no winner.

Don't become defensive or try to solicit guilt. "How can you say those things to me after all I've done for you . . . ??" This response only escalates the situation. Don't be afraid to assert yourself.

Don't get dragged down. Screaming and name-calling only fan the flames. Take the high road.

DO:

Slow things down. Take her aside and calmly say, "I know you're very angry with me for not letting you stay out. But now you need to listen to me. First, it's OK for you to be angry, but it's not OK for you to talk to me like that. You can say the same thing without raising your voice or using bad language."

Be consistent and firm in your convictions. "Your curfew is ten tonight and you need to respect my decision." Kids need limits. This is how they learn to limit and discipline themselves.

Consider reasonable options. Hold firm but offer several acceptable home-based options. "I'd be willing to rent you guys a video you can watch when you come home." Or, "It's OK with me if you want to stay at Susie's house but you still need to be in by ten."

Firm yet calm responses from you allow your child to cool down and get with the program. Your child will feel safe expressing her anger and disagreeing with you, and learn how to do it constructively. In this way children learn that they can be very angry with the people they love and still respectfully disagree.

PICK UP DISTRESS SIGNALS

Most kids send out signals when something is really upsetting them. It's our job to read them. But sometimes our radar is down. We're too stressed, too busy, or too upset ourselves to notice. Other times, we ask if they're OK but get hit with "Fine, now leave me alone," and we allow ourselves to be talked out of our concern. Here are ten signals that indicate you need to initiate a talk to find out what's bothering your child.

1. **Your child is not acting "herself."** Something is different. She may be hanging around or clinging to you, crying, sulking, or doing other things to draw your attention.

2. **He is overly defensive or hostile** when you ask, "Is anything wrong?"

3. **She becomes uncharacteristically quiet** or excessively angry over minor things.

4. **He is retreating deeper and deeper into a fantasy world**—of violent video games, horror films, or heavy metal music—and is unreachable.

5. **She pushes you away, complaining,** "Just leave me alone!"

6. **He says and/or does radical things** that are actually calls for help and attention.

7. **She has a look of desperation,** appears spaced out, drugged, or drunk.

8. **He always seems irritable** and on the verge of being upset.

9. **He is testing you at every turn** and is becoming a disciplinary problem.

10. **She denies there's a problem** when something is obviously bothering her.

TUNE IN TO YOUR CHILD

You've picked up a signal. Now what?

Step 1 is to find out what's going on. Say you've picked up a signal that your son is very upset. You've gotten wind from his little sister that he was threatened by another student at school. He is afraid and doesn't want to go back to school. He's also been thinking about bringing a knife to school. You might get a conversation going by asking:

■ "You're my son, I can usually tell when something is bothering you. Is there something going on you want to tell me about?"

■ "What is the best way for you to protect yourself from the boy who threatened you?"

■ "So you're thinking about not going to school. Or carrying a knife in case you need to protect yourself."

Step 2 is thinking out loud and developing a strategy. Tune in to what's causing your child to be scared or angry and help him deal with it. Help him get control of the beliefs and perceptions that fuel anger or fear. To this end, you might ask: "Can we talk about other things you might do to protect yourself?"

Help your child figure out his options and review the pros and cons. Find out what he is doing about it. He may already be handling the situation effectively and just needs to be encouraged. He may come to you for "coaching" about what to do. *Listen first.* After your son has his say, ask him how you can help.

Step 3 is to take action and follow through with the plan. See Chapter 6 for a full explanation of how to help your child deal with a threat of violence.

"HELLLOOO?"

Let's face it. Sometimes our children can't get through to us. Perhaps we're too caught up in the rush of our own lives, too tired or distracted at the end of the day. Or we're not up to listening to anybody else's problems. Or we just don't get it.

Ask your child, "Are there times you want to talk to me and just can't get through?" If she says "Yes," apologize and tell her you are learning to be a better listener. Give her your 100 percent attention. Face her, make eye contact, and don't interrupt. In fact, come up with a "code" she can use to get you to stop whatever you're doing or saying and tune in to her. A group of high school students I met with recently suggested some lines kids might use to get their parents' attention. Review these with your child and see which ones work best for both of you:

- "Mom, I'm trying to tell you something. Can we talk?"

- "Dad, I know you're busy but can you give me a few minutes? Please don't 'later' me. This is really important."

- "Mom, it's my time! It's my turn to get your undivided attention."

- "Dad, I need to talk to you. I want you to just listen.

- "Oops, you did it again! It feels like you're only half-listening."

- "Dad, I'm getting really frustrated. Every time I bring this up, you yell at me. Can't we take turns talking and listening to each other?"

- "I'm having a really tough time right now. I need you guys."

- "Mom, it's like you're not taking what I say seriously. Can you be a little more understanding?"

Reality Check We all miss cues. When you realize you missed a signal, go back to your kid and say, "I'm sorry I didn't tune in when you mentioned [the problem]. Can we make a time to talk?" Children appreciate when we come to them and apologize. Yours will probably let you slide. In time your radar will improve.

THE BEST (AND WORST) TIMES TO TALK

Sometimes the moment for discussion just presents itself. Other times, you must make a conversation happen. Here are some do's and don'ts to help you choose the right moment for your talk and how to get started.

DON'T:	DO:
Don't wait until you're in the heat of the moment to bring things up.	Begin cultivating a family routine of talking things out right away.
Don't bring up potentially embarrassing things in front of her siblings or friends.	Take it slow and realize you may have to find the right time to talk.
Don't try to force a conversation when he is clearly upset and not ready to talk.	Tell him how much you appreciate his trust and honesty.
Don't expect or pressure your child to open up all at once.	Be sensitive to how much privacy she needs to open up.
Don't try to talk when it's late at night or with the TV on in the background.	Ask, "Is this a good time to talk?" Give him your undivided attention.
Don't speak in a harsh, critical, or nagging tone.	Be patient. Relax your face and voice.

ONE GOOD TALK LEADS TO ANOTHER

If your child comes to you upset and leaves feeling better—or at least understood—chances are she'll come back again to talk. Build on those successes.

Here are other ways to jump-start a meaningful conversation and deepen your relationship with your child:

■ **Have a "silent conversation."** When my kids were feeling blue, I'd sometimes just go into their room and hang out with them or bring them a snack. These "house calls" and silent conversations sent the unspoken message, "I know you're down. I'm here for you. If you want to talk, I'm listening, but we don't need to say anything."

- **Do a *Back to the Future* flashback.** Ask what your child thinks you were like in high school. Ask your son, "How would I have fit in at your school? How are things different today?" Have fun with this. You'll learn a lot about how your child fits in and the daily challenges he faces trying to be a part of the school community.

- **Ask your child his or her opinion** on something you're struggling with—this does not include deeply personal issues such as marriage, divorce, sex, or depression. Keep it simple and G-rated. Say you're watching wrestling on TV. Somebody is pounding on someone's head with a chair. Tell your child that you enjoy watching but feel uneasy being entertained at the expense of someone getting hurt. Sharing our conflicts and dilemmas with our kids opens the door for our children to share theirs with us.

- **Admit that you handled a situation poorly.** You became impatient and yelled at your eighty year-old mother, argued with a coworker over something unimportant, or fought with a neighbor over something minor. Now you recognize that if you had it to do over again you would handle it better, and that you owe someone an apology. Admitting mistakes paves the way for your child to tell you about a situation he handled poorly and fixing it.

RAISING CONFIDENT CHILDREN

Respectfully listening and talking to our kids is a powerful form of violence prevention. Knowing how to ask good questions is a skill you can acquire. When we talk to our kids about what's weighing heavily on *their* minds, our children not only unburden themselves but they learn new coping skills, and self-control. Reaching out to us as parents is also their basis for trusting authority. This trust and respect will translate into going to a trusted teacher or a counselor with problems they can't handle alone. As we will see, our children's own ability to listen is a tool they can use for diffusing potentially violent situations in the future.

CHAPTER **4**

CRIMES IN SAN DIEGO OCCUR WHEN KIDS HAVE BEEN DRINKING AND/OR USING DRUGS.—*SDDA* ■ BULLYING

IS INCREASINGLY VIEWED AS AN IMPORTANT CONTRIBUTOR TO YOUTH VIOLENCE, INCLUDING HOMICIDE AND

THE

SUICIDE.—*GCU* ■ 1.6 MILLION CHILDREN IN GRADES 6 THROUGH 10 ARE BULLIED ONCE A WEEK OR MORE OFTEN,

ANATOMY

AND 1.7 MILLION ARE BULLYING OTHERS THAT FREQUENTLY.—*NICHD* ■ APPROXIMATELY ONE HALF OF ALL HOMES

OF

IN THE UNITED STATES CONTAIN A FIREARM.—*AACAP* ■ SELF-DESTRUCTIVE AND SUICIDAL BEHAVIOR OFTEN

VIOLENCE

ACCOMPANY SCHOOL VIOLENCE.—*US DOH* ■ SUICIDE IS CURRENTLY THE THIRD LEADING CAUSE OF DEATH

IN CHILDREN.—*US DOH* ■ STUDENT HOMICIDES AND SUICIDES ARE FOUND TO BE MOST PREVALENT AFTER SUMMER

OR WINTER BREAKS.—*CDC[1]* ■ 9% OF EXPELLED ELEMENTARY SCHOOL STUDENTS ARE REMOVED FOR BRINGING

FIREARMS TO SCHOOL.—*US DOE[1]* ■ A 3-YEAR OLD CHILD HAS THE FINGER STRENGTH TO PULL A TRIGGER.—*NFCCHM*

With the school shootings of recent years still fresh in our minds, symbolizing what every parent fears for their children, we're all engaged in the struggle to understand what causes this frightening new kind of youth violence.

The first place we have to look is at ourselves—the way we live, the choices we make in reacting to life's injustices, and the animosity and anger we harbor. We're all "wired" differently. Some of us have short fuses. We're easily provoked and have bad tempers. Others are more easygoing. We don't seem to let things get to us. Still others keep things bottled up inside, and it may be just a waiting game until these emotions explode.

Given enough anger, all of us are capable of "losing it" and becoming aggressive . . . even violent. We strike out and strike back when we feel hurt or cornered or threatened. Some people turn their anger on themselves, and become self-destructive or suicidal.

HOW HURT BECOMES ANGER

Anger is a way of expressing unresolved pain. When something has hurt us, we feel slighted, cheated, or betrayed, and our pain seeks an outlet. We need a release, to cry out or to talk about it. If there's no outlet and the pain persists, the pain that's not being "listened to" builds into anger. For some of us this occurs at lightning speed.

These emotions can get bottled up inside us, and often we don't know what to do. It's the same with our kids. Ideally, they know how to help themselves before their hurt turns to anger. They'll have healthy and constructive outlets. They'll come to us when they're hurt or scared. In reality, however, not many kids walk up to their parents and say, "Please help me. I'm losing it!"

Most kids express their emotions indirectly. They "act out" their anger. For example, they lash out at others, defy authority, or destroy property. Or they hide their emotions by shutting themselves inside their rooms. What you see on the surface isn't the real problem, of course. But how do you connect to find out what the real problem is? And how can a parent tell when a child is hurting so much that anger itself is becoming a problem?

ROOT CAUSES OF VIOLENCE

Anger shows itself in many forms, any of which can lead to violence. The underlying causes can be broken down further to better understand violence.

- **Fear.** Violence can be a reaction to fear. When we perceive a threat, either real or imagined, we instinctively protect ourselves. We want to get it before it gets us. Violent kids are often scared kids, who strike out first because they feel cornered or afraid. Anger can be easier to express than fear—especially for men, who believe that fear is a sign of weakness.

- **Revenge.** To someone who feels victimized by an injustice, "payback" through violence may seem like the only way.

- **Hatred.** Violence grows out of hatred. Hatred is often born, cultivated, and fueled by deeply held resentments between members of different racial, ethnic, and religious groups. Minorities and gay and lesbian children are often targets for mean-spiritedness because they are "different," and that stirs up a lot of uneasy feelings in some people.

- **Jealousy.** Too often we hear and read of violence born of a "jealous rage." Feelings of rejection, loss, and betrayal can become so intense and overwhelming, that people become desperate, they lose it.

- **Peer pressure.** Violence can be a means to achieve peer status when a child reaches adolescence. Gangs are an extreme example of this. A violent act is often required as a rite of passage for a boy or girl to be accepted into the group.

- **Psychological or emotional disturbance.** Diagnosable mental or emotional problems may be accompanied by excessive hostility, a lack of conscience, and a disregard for others.

- **Hereditary factors.** Biological makeup also plays a role. Some of us are born with "short fuses" and impulsiveness, factors that can lead to violent behavior.

- **Abuse and neglect.** Physical and sexual abuse are often transmitted from one generation to another. Violent behavior is sometimes the only behavior a child knows.

HIGH-RISK FACTORS

Kids act violently for a variety of other reasons that are learned, or acquired in their environment. Here are the leading risk indicators for violence and suggestions for dealing with them.

DRUGS AND ALCOHOL

Alcohol lowers teenage inhibitions. "Liquid courage" gives kids enough false bravery to instigate fights, or worse. The behaviors and emotions that kids would normally be able to control are amplified. Drugs can produce the same effects, often in ways that can be harder for a parent to detect, which means educating yourself about drugs that are available to your children.

You must have "the talk" with your children about the dangers of drugs and alcohol. Even though your kids may have heard it a thousand times on TV and in school, you must find out: Is your child drinking or taking drugs? Even if your child claims (swears!) to be alcohol and drug-free, it is your job to monitor the situation. Use your eyes, ears, and nose to detect alcohol, marijuana, or other drugs. Our homes need to be sobriety checkpoints.

Signs your child is using drugs or drinking:

- **Looks different.** Red, puffy eyes, a glazed or "stoned" look, dilated pupils, runny nose, coughing or tremors (shaking).

- **Acts different.** Moody, irritable, hostile, or oddly brash.

- **Loses interest** in school, hobbies, sports, appearance, and old friends.

- **Trouble concentrating.** Poor attention span. Falls behind in school.

- **Hangs out with the "wrong" kids and stays out very late.**

- **Withdraws.** Always wants to be left alone. Closes self in room.

- **Always tired.** Sleeps a lot. No energy.

Keeping your children drug and alcohol free:

- **Set an example.** Be drug- and alcohol-free yourself. Get help for other kinds of addictive behaviors like smoking, gambling, overeating, and spending.

- **Make a "substance-free" agreement** with your child. (*See Online Resource Directory.*)

- **Confront your child's drug and alcohol use.** If your child breaks a "substance-free" agreement, you must take action. Have a serious heart-to-heart talk or see a substance abuse counselor to assess the problem. Monitor your child until the situation is under control and take whatever steps are necessary to prevent drug and alcohol problems from developing.

- **Engage her in fun activities** such as athletics, outdoor recreation, volunteer work, and hobbies. (*See Online Resource Directory for a complete list of community activities and resources.*)

- **Encourage your child to hang out with kids who are alcohol/drug-free** in alcohol/drug-free environments. Being around other kids who are drinking and "using" makes it more likely your child will try alcohol and drugs. Drug dealers and the drug business breed only danger and violence. Innocent kids can get caught in the crossfire.

- **Have a firm "no drinking and driving" pact.** Don't hand your child the keys to the family car if you have any doubts he can keep his promise not to drink and drive. Don't allow him to drive with friends until he agrees not to get in the car of someone who has been using drugs or drinking. Look him in the eyes and get his 100% agreement. Keeping our kids safe also means keeping all drivers sober and "straight."

- **Make your home kid-friendly and comfortable.** Kids need a safe, supervised hangout where they can relax with their buddies, have fun, do homework, eat pizza, talk openly, play, create— and air out their problems. A place where they can be kids.

BULLIES

No one likes a bully. Bullies pick on weaker kids and can make their victims' lives miserable to the point they don't want to go to school. If you suspect your child is being bullied, sit him down and ask him outright. Be patient. You're bringing up a painful and humiliating subject. If your child won't talk to you about it, it might be easier for him to talk to his big brother or sister, or other parent, cousin, teacher, counselor, mentor, or adult friend. In any case, act immediately to end your child's victimization and prevent further injury. Details on how to approach this are provided in Chapter 6.

Every bully has his day and eventually can become a target himself. Parents often learn their children are bullying other kids when they get a call from school or another child's parents. If you suspect your child is threatening or picking on other kids, here are some ways to intervene:

- **Get the facts.** If your child won't tell you, talk to other parents, teachers, and possibly the victim and/or the victim's parents.

- **Your child should apologize** to his victim and undo any damage to the extent it's possible. For example, if your child destroyed the victim's headphones, he must replace them.

- **Help your child understand** that physical and/or emotional abuse of another person is never acceptable.

- **If your child hangs out with other bullies,** you should separate him from that group. Driving your child home after school rather than letting him spend time with the other bullies is one way. Another is finding positive after-school activities that help him get back on the right side of the fence.

- **Let your child talk about the fears and insecurities** that might be causing him to act like a bully. Make an "action plan" to address those problems, like going for counseling or taking an anger management or anti-bullying class.

GANGS

Gangs are a frightening reality—even in some elementary and middle schools. To keep your children safe from gangs, learn about gang activity in your area. Help your child avoid gang members and hangouts whenever possible. If your own or someone else's child is being threatened or harassed by a gang, consult the gang-prevention specialist at your local police department (there usually is one). He will help you plot a safe strategy to get the kids out of harm's way. This is not something you should try to handle yourself. (For more about how to make your child's world safe from gangs, see Chapter 5.)

TRUANCY

Truancy is one of the first signs a child may be headed for trouble. Hundreds of thousands of children are absent from our nation's schools each day. Where are these kids? Often on the streets—getting into trouble. They're not in class learning; they're falling further and further behind. When kids skip school and parents fail to act, it sets in motion a downward slide to disappointment, failure, dropping out, and even arrests. Keeping kids in school lowers the juvenile crime rate and prepares kids to take their place in society.

BOREDOM

Some children have a knack for staying active; they find things to do and enjoy doing them. Other kids can't seem to find anything "fun" to keep them interested, occupied, and out of trouble. It is said, "Idle hands are the devil's workshop." If your child hasn't found after-school activities he or she enjoys, get busy. For ideas, consult your local YMCA, Boys or Girls Club, community recreation center, parks department, school district, church or synagogue youth group leader—and let your child choose one that appeals. Requiring kids to participate in three to four hours of after-school programs every week doesn't make you a dictator. Seeing them discover things they enjoy and keeping them off the streets will make it well worth the effort.

POVERTY AND ENVIRONMENT

Kids brought up in poor neighborhoods are often surrounded by violence. Breaking the vicious cycle of poverty and violence means providing healthy outlets and activities for these children. This involves bringing resources and programs into low-income areas. A study in the troubled South Central section of Los Angeles found that kids who succeed had two things going for them; a sixth-grade reading level and a consistent parent in their lives.

IMPULSIVENESS

Most kids learn to curb childhood impulsiveness. They develop self-control. Children who have impulse-control and/or concentration problems often have trouble adjusting to school and society. The impulse to strike out or strike back when something hurts or disrespects—"disses"—them, combined with feelings of inadequacy and rejection, makes them susceptible to violence. If you're concerned that impulsive, temperamental behavior could get your son or daughter in trouble, consult a child psychologist to determine whether a learning or behavior problem, or a neurological problem like ADD (Attention-Deficiency Disorder) is the cause. Or, a psychologist can suggest what you can do to help solve your child's impulsive behavior.

BEING A SMART ALECK

It's one thing to be funny, and humor is a wonderful thing, but sarcasm and mean-spirited wit can become a liability. If your child has a tendency to be a smart aleck, to "mouth off" or make fun of people, talk about how in the wrong situation this can get a person into trouble. An innocent joke or remark directed at the wrong people, at the wrong time, can have treacherous results. A wise-cracking teenager in suburban Detroit was recently beaten to death by four gang members he had taunted as they drove past his friend's party earlier that evening.

CHOICE OF FRIENDS

Kids who get hurt as a result of violence are often innocent bystanders in the wrong place at the wrong time. Their only mistake was being with friends whose high-risk behavior placed them in harm's way. You can't choose your child's friends or control their social lives. But you can do a variety of things to help them make good choices. Here are some of them:

- **Show confidence in your child** and what you have taught her about right and wrong. Tell her you know it's not always easy to make good choices but that you trust her. Let your kid know she's "innocent until proven guilty."

- **Remember when you were a teenager.** Having friends and being included means everything to kids. Being an understanding parent will go a long way to keeping your relationship strong.

- **Proceed with caution.** Talking about your child's friends is a highly sensitive topic. If you're going to inquire, do so in a noncritical manner. Think about what you're going to say before saying it.

- **Get to know their friends,** especially the "bad" ones.

- **Ask them to tell you about friends** they consider good influences and friends who live "on the edge."

- **Express your preferences for the friends you like** without mentioning the ones you don't like.

- **Set limits on at-risk friendships and behaviors.** Sometimes it's necessary to lay down the law when your child is not making good decisions about friends. Children must learn that bad decisions have negative consequences.

Remember, timing is everything. Go slow and easy. Keep things in perspective. Making statements or asking questions about friends is most effective after you've opened the lines of communication.

LOOKING DIFFERENT

Talking to your child about appearance is another one of those very sticky subjects. Sometimes our children unwittingly make themselves targets of other kids by their dress, their hair, their "look." Extreme clothes and hairstyles are innocent expressions of their individuality and creativity. Dying hair blue or green is also their way of rebelling. Children dressing in black leather and chains, or heavily tattooed and pierced, are making a more serious kind of statement. They may be using their appearance as a means of intimidation, or to make an aggressive statement.

Looking different can be perceived in extremely hostile ways by other groups of children. Clothing, colors, and slang words take on different meanings in different neighborhoods. A kid who wears baggy jeans and gang colors because it's the cool thing to do in his suburban high school could be putting his life at risk if he wanders into another neighborhood and is mistaken for a gang member.

The solution is not to make our children look like every other child. Nor is it to dictate what they wear. We want our kids to express themselves as individuals, and we want to teach them tolerance for others. At the point that their safety is at risk, talk with them about their appearance. Say their fashion choices are resulting in taunting at school. Explore with them how they might be making themselves targets by sending out a message of "I'm tougher/cooler/better than you . . ." or, "This is my turf." Explain how this can provoke taunting and, in some cases, violent confrontation. If the problem persists, you may need to draw the line insisting on beautiful blond hair by week's end (that is, get rid of the blue hair!).

THE FAMILY COMPUTER

Like any tool, a computer can be a blessing or a danger to our children. Kids use the Internet to research term papers or learn how to build bombs, to communicate with their grandparents or interact with strangers (sometimes sexual predators), to buy books or buy guns. Set firm limits on the use of the Internet with these rules for safe surfing:

- Never give out identifying information (i.e., name, address or telephone number).

- Don't tell other kids your screen name password.

- Never respond to negative, obscene, or threatening communications.

- Notify proper authorities about websites promoting violence or illegal activity at www.wiasa.org, or similar websites.

- Sign a family contract for online safety.

- Be respectful and considerate to other Web surfers.

See Online Resource Directory for more information on computer safety.

SELF-DESTRUCTIVE AND SUICIDAL BEHAVIOR

Self-destructive and suicidal behavior often accompany school violence. Consider the two Columbine students who took their own lives after killing 13 people and wounding 23 others. Helping a suicidal child may prevent an act of violence against himself or others.

Six signs of a child being suicidal:

1. **Describes intent and a method** when asked if he's considering suicide.

2. **Appears depressed, angry,** and unable to enjoy life.

3. **Preoccupied with death and dying.**

4. Drops out of usual activities.

5. Gives away prized possessions.

6. Physical symptoms like weight loss, can't sleep, etc.

Many kids think about suicide at some time or another. If you have even the slightest suspicion your child is considering suicide, you must ask, "Are you thinking of taking your own life?" If your child answers "yes," here's what to do and not do:

DON'T:

Don't get angry with your child.

Don't threaten her or get into a fight.

Don't try to psychoanalyze him.

Don't make it about you by falling apart emotionally or blaming yourself.

Don't leave your child's side until he's OK. Don't let him push you away until a clear plan to get help is in place.

Don't panic!

DO:

Remain as calm as possible and thank him for telling you.

Talk with your child about why she is feeling suicidal.

Just listen.

Lend an understanding ear. Show her your love and concern.

Make a "no suicide" verbal agreement with your child and accompany him to a counselor's office for immediate help.

Find out what she has planned. Calmly remove any weapons or and/or dangerous drugs from the house. Call 911 or the police department if he has put himself in imminent danger.

See Online Resource Directory for more information on suicide prevention.

ACCESS TO GUNS

Children bring handguns to school every day. The *good* news is, thanks to increased emphasis on teaching gun safety, fatal gun accidents among children declined 84 percent in the past twenty-five years. Whether or not you own a gun, talking to your child about gun safety is a must. Have this talk as soon as possible.

Young children need to learn the difference between guns used on TV for entertainment, toy guns used for play, and real guns. Your child also needs to learn what to do if he comes upon a gun. The Eddie Eagle GunSafe® Program—a top-rated gun safety program—offers four simple guidelines for children twelve and under:

1. Stop!

2. Don't touch.

3. Leave the area.

4. Tell an adult.

The most important rules are the first two: "Stop" and "Don't Touch." After that, children then must resist their natural curiosity and "Leave the Area," whether it be a playground or a living room. Lastly, they need to "Tell an Adult." If you or their guardian is not available, they must go to a trusted neighbor, relative, or teacher. If a trusted adult is not available they should call 911.

As your children grow older, they must continue learning age-appropriate safety guidelines, including when and how they may use a gun. Parents who own guns must teach their children about state and federal laws on gun ownership, storage, purchase, and transport. If you're not up to speed on the laws in your state or qualified to talk about gun safety with your child, consult the NRA or local police department. Instruct your child as to the specific circumstances under which he may use and not use a gun:

When Not to Use	**When to Use**
When you don't have my permission. Never in school or on school grounds. It's the law!	When you have my permission. Only in a safe, appropriate setting.
If you have not received proper training and supervision.	After you have been properly trained and supervised in gun use and safety training.
Casually in play, for showing off, as part of a potentially dangerous game, or as an instrument of anger, revenge, power, or retribution.	For sport (hunting, target shooting, etc.) when you have proper training and a license.
When you have not yet learned about the safety features of a particular gun from me or a certified instructor.	After I show you how to safely handle this gun. Some guns have safety pins to indicate a bullet in the chamber and some don't. Each gun must be handled differently.

Gun accidents and homicides account for preventable deaths of children every year. Guns cannot be left freely accessible to children. Never store firearms (loaded or not) or storage keys where children of any age can find them. Talk with your children about the responsibilities and dangers of firearms. Explain that they are never to be touched without your express permission, and tell them you expect them to abide by your rules religiously. Beyond these basics of gun safety, how much you want your child to learn about guns is your choice.

Parents who don't own guns must still educate their children about gun safety. Chances are, your child will be exposed to guns, possibly at a friend's house, a party, or even at school. Knowing about gun safety could save theirs or somebody else's life. It is every parents' responsibility to teach their child gun safety, and how to handle a gun if you own one. (*See the Online Resource Directory for further guidelines about gun safety and The Eddie Eagle GunSafe® Program.*)

COPYCAT VIOLENCE

Violence can also result from "copycat" behavior. Copycats imitate highly publicized acts of violence or threaten similar acts. Parents who notice warning signs of copycat behavior, such as verbal threats of wanting to "do the same thing" or an unusual fascination with a violent incident (like a school shooting), should immediately consult an expert to have their child evaluated. More warning signs of a potentially violent child are found in Chapter 10.

SPIRITUAL EMPTINESS

Kids with no hope, faith, direction, or remorse have nothing to lose by acting indiscriminately. Life must have meaning. Part of our children's spiritual survival is to believe in something bigger than what's happening that moment. For some, this is God, a Higher Power, or Creator. For others, it is nature and love that give life meaning. And yet, so many children seem to have little or nothing to believe in. They are lost and devoid of feeling. Their world is dark and they don't seem to care about anything. They don't feel their lives have any purpose.

How do kids become so empty? Often it's because they have been badly hurt and disappointed. They have given up on people, especially adults, and given up on themselves. It's safer to feel nothing, to not care and "numb out." At least they won't have to suffer any further pain or disappointment.

Contemporary inspirational music and books, youth programs and retreats, Bible study groups, and houses of worship are some of the places our children can find spiritual fulfillment. Inspirational youth activity programs like *Motivating the Teen Spirit* and school-based programs like "Passages" help children's spiritual development restore a sense of hope and purpose to their lives. (*See Online Resource Directory for details.*)

NOBODY CARES

The presence of an adult who cares is a universally recognized component of every child's survival and success. Kids who do not have the active involvement of a parent, teacher, mentor, or significant adult family member in their lives are often lost and unhappy. They can be the most susceptible to violence, either as a perpetrator or victim. Children who are lost emotionally need someone to take them under their wing and work with them. Although they may appear down and out, and have a long road of healing ahead, a spark of hope from someone who believes in them can change everything. Children can be amazingly resilient.

Churches, youth organizations, mentor programs, social service agencies, and parent effectiveness classes are available in most every community to help you and to help your child.

THE PROCESS OF VIOLENCE PREVENTION

The road to preventing youth violence begins early. It starts with recognizing when kids are hurting, addressing the source of their pain or fear—then taking the steps to provide them with healthy outlets for their emotions. In addition to anger, out-of-control emotions like hatred, jealousy, and revenge lead to violence. Factors that increase the possibility of violence include drugs and alcohol, suicidal and impulsive behavior, access to guns, spiritual emptiness, and the absence of a caring adult.

Try as we might, some kids become hardened—their pain becomes bitterness, and violent behavior is their payback. These children seize power through intimidation and retribution, and strike back at classmates, teachers, and a world they feel has wronged them. They don't seem to care what happens to themselves or others.

Mercifully, the human spirit is such that most deep wounds can heal, anger can be released, and violence can be averted. Constructive ways of expressing anger, hurt, fear, rage, and despair can be taught. As violence prevention becomes a top priority in our homes and in our nation, we make our children's—and grandchildren's—world a safer place.

CHAPTER **5**

FFENSES IN 90% OF CASES. —*NYS/NIH* ■ REPORTED BIAS CRIME VICTIMS IN 1995: 10,469. —*FBI*[2] ■ ALMOST HALF

F MIDDLE AND HIGH SCHOOL PUPILS ADMITTED STEALING FROM A STORE DURING THE YEAR; 25% SAID THEY

THE

ID SO AT LEAST TWICE.—*JIE* ■ BULLYING PREVENTION PROGRAMS IN SEVERAL ELEMENTARY AND JUNIOR

PARENT'S

IGH SCHOOLS CUT BULLYING IN HALF, DECREASED THEFT, VANDALISM, AND TRUANCY, AND IMPROVED THE

VIOLENCE-

CHOOL'S SOCIAL CLIMATE.—*USSG*[1] ■ PROGRAMS THAT FOCUS ON BUILDING A SCHOOL'S CAPACITY TO PLAN,

PREVENTION

MPLEMENT, AND SUSTAIN POSITIVE CHANGES CAN SIGNIFICANTLY REDUCE STUDENT DELINQUENCY AND

TOOLBOX

RUG USE.—*USSG*[1] ■ HIGH SCHOOL ATHLETES FIND DRUGS JUST AS ACCESSIBLE AS THEIR NON-ATHLETIC

EERS, BUT USE DRUGS LESS.—*JIE* ■ THE AMERICAN ACADEMY OF PEDIATRICS CALLED FOR VIOLENCE-

REVENTION COUNSELING AND SCREENING TO BECOME PART OF A CHILD'S ROUTINE VISIT TO THE DOCTOR.—*ABC*

Supervising every moment of our children's lives, protecting them from every danger, controlling their every move, is a recipe for madness. It cannot be done! Nor should it be attempted. Children, like their parents, are going to make mistakes and grow from them. What we *can* do is to afford our children every protection and safeguard against danger and violence. To do this, we need the right tools.

10 ESSENTIAL TOOLS TO PROTECT YOUR CHILD

1. **Know where your child is.** Pretty basic, isn't it? But sometimes we forget. Have your kids check in regularly. Set and enforce reasonable curfews. Pat them on the back when they come home on time—and discipline them when they don't.

2. **Know your child's friends.** You can learn a lot about your children by their friends. Ask yourself:

   - "Who are my child's friends?" Knowing who your child's friends are provides a much fuller picture of your child's world. Not knowing is very risky.

   - "Are her friends comfortable around me?" How your child's friends act toward you—open or secretive—may tell you a lot about them.

   - "Could I be more positive and friendly toward my child's friends?" Being approachable makes you "cool," as does making your home a welcoming place.

   - "How could I get my child's friends to talk to me more?" Asking about their interests and their families is a starting point. Use open-ended questions and get to know them.

   - "What are his friend's favorite things to do?" Knowing this gives you an edge in planning fun and interesting activities and outings for your kids and their friends. Keeping your child and his friends engaged in healthy activities is the goal.

3. **Get to know the parents** of your child's friends, and enemies. Establishing a direct line of communication with the parents of his friends can provide helpful feedback about how he acts when he is not with you, as well as provide mutual support and much-needed cooperation in times of crisis. Knowing the parents of his "enemies" might provide valuable information that could help avert trouble ahead.

4. **Build your child's confidence.** Confidence is often the best form of self-defense. Kids who believe in themselves usually don't want to hurt anyone. Confidence and self-esteem can also be a deterrent to would-be bullies. But these qualities need to be fed regularly. If your child's self-esteem is running low, consider these confidence-builders:

    ■ *Listen* **to your child's thoughts and ideas.** Your willingness to listen to what she's saying and your compliments may work like magic.

    ■ **Treat your child with respect.** Make certain the rest of the family does the same. If a child is constantly criticized at home, his self-esteem suffers. Parents who lose their tempers and harshly criticize need to get it under control or risk damaging their children's confidence.

    ■ **Remind your child that self-worth is ours alone—** it can't be taken from us without our permission. Neither can our honor. People may try to make us feel bad, they will bait us—and this happens a lot in school. We need to remember that it's not about us. It's about the other person.

Reality Check As you open yourself to your child's world and that of their friends, you may experience that all-too-common "Where have I been?" feeling. You may be shocked and surprised by your "baby." Now she's dating, reading the classics, and discussing her future. Don't beat yourself up for being so out of touch. Listen and learn. Your baby is growing up.

- **Encourage your child to join an activity group or athletic team** and work on developing his skills. Doing builds confidence.

- **Have your child take karate classes,** not so much for self-defense as self-esteem. Knowing they have the ability to fight back and protect themselves is self-assuring for kids.

5. **Set healthy limits.** From the moment we begin teaching them not to touch the stove, play in the street, talk to strangers, or fool with matches, we are setting limits for our children. Their very survival depends on it. We protect our kids when they are young— until they're mature enough to take care of themselves.

Kids experiment with new freedoms as they get older. It's natural for them to spread their wings. Our job is to provide safe ways to do this—which can be extremely challenging when fast cars, smoking, drinking, drugs, sex, and violence are glamorized in our society.

But how do you provide safe ways for your child to test and expand their limits? How do you get your kids to obey the speed limit, stay drug- and alcohol-free, avoid dangerous neighborhoods, avoid kids who are bad influences, and all the other "at-risk" behaviors without making them feel like you're babying, insulting, or distrusting them?

Setting limits is tough but necessary. It requires strength, conviction, and persistence, as well as the willingness to be thought of as the "bad guy" by your once-adoring child. Unpopular as it might make you to forbid your thirteen-year-old from going to a hard rock concert, or tell him he can no longer hang out with a certain friend, or that he's grounded, it beats the alternative—your child being unsafe or getting hurt.

At that very moment your children may resent, even hate you for restricting them. But they need you to set limits until they're mature enough to make good judgments on their own. Childhood shouldn't be rushed. Trust, freedom, responsibility, and privileges need to be earned. Years from now, your kids may tell you they were relieved you made these decisions because it made it easier to say "no" to their friends.

Here are indispensable guidelines for setting limits that protect your child:

- **Be proactive.** Talk to your child about rules and responsibilities before there's a crisis, or a problem. Do it when you're calm and keep it positive. Remember, this is not about punishment, it's about safety. Do not approach your child in anger or in a panic.

- **Be specific.** Clarify exactly what your child can and cannot do. Don't leave it open to interpretation. Write down all of the rules, as well as the consequences for not following them. Give a copy to your child so there will be no misunderstandings.

- **Be positive.** Express your concerns for her safety, but do not unload your personal fears and anxieties on your child. Blanket statements indicting all her friends as bad influences, threats about taking away all her privileges, or trashing the ethnic or racial groups she hangs out with will only make her defensive and less inclined to "open up" to you.

- **Be consistent.** Kids learn best from consistency. Parents who cave in, use rules as bargaining chips, or frequently change rules send the wrong message. Their kids can grow up thinking they can manipulate authority figures and avoid the consequences of their behavior. Stand firm, day after day—no matter how much your child might beg or plead. Rules are rules, and the consequences for not following them should be clear and consistently carried out by you.

- **Be firm but respectful.** State your case but allow time for your child to express his thoughts and ideas about family rules and limits. Assure him that the rules will change as he gets older and proves himself capable of making good decisions.

Reality Check Some of us are just born tough. When it comes to doling out discipline and "tough love," we're right at home. And some of us are softies. A little guilt, pressure, and a "Pleeeze, Mom?"—and we give in. Good parenting requires a little of both. We need to be a drill sergeant and a best friend. Parenting isn't an exact science. Just do your best to balance when to lighten up and when to get tough.

6. **Make your child accountable.** To foster a sense of responsibility in our children, we need to involve them in the decisions affecting them. Say your child has gotten into another fight and is on the verge of being suspended from school. Something has to change. There have to be consequences, but there also has to be a plan for changing his behavior. Providing him with alternatives gives him the power to decide from choices that are acceptable to you. You might say: "I'm going to suggest some alternatives. You can attend an anger management program, you can work with a therapist, or there's a book on controlling emotions we can read together. It's your choice." Once he has made his choice, he has agreed to take responsibility for his violent behavior in a way that is mutually acceptable.

7. **Become better informed about school safety.** Schedule time with the principal, the school safety and security officer, or your child's teacher. Remember, most schools have thousands of students. Good timing, patience, and respect will get you information and answers.

   ■ Find out which school safety laws and policies are already enforced in your child's school district.

   ■ Find out what's being done currently to make your child's school a safer place. What's planned for the future? (more security staff, anti-bullying programs, bond issues for school construction, cameras in classrooms?)

   ■ Familiarize yourself with other people, organizations, and programs that share your concerns for safe schools.

   ■ Get names from your children's school of people whose job is violence prevention. Who's in charge? Does the school have a safety director and a security officer?

   ■ Find out if your child's school has identified individuals and or groups who may pose a threat to the safety of your child or others. If so, what is being done?

- What resources are there in your school district to assist at-risk children?

- What relationship does your children's school have with the local police?

8. **Talk to your kids about the threat of violence.**
    Let your child know you're interested and want to know more about the risks of violence in their school.

    Ask these questions:

    - "Have there been threats or actual acts of violence at school?"

    - "Are there racial or gang tensions at school?"

    - "Do you know kids who have access to guns or other weapons?"

    - "Do you know students who have actually brought guns to school?"

    - "How does the school address the gun issue?"

    - "Are the police ever present at your school? If so, what are their responsibilities to maintain safety?"

    - "What will happen if there is a crisis at the school and the police have to be called in?"

9. **Get involved at school.** Once you and your children are better informed about what's happening at their school, become more involved. The best schools are those where parents and students work together. Review the following list of school safety programs. Find the ones that appeal to you, and pitch in.

    - **Ask your children.** Ask them to recommend how you can become more involved in preventing violence at their school. Ask their teachers and principal.

    - **Participate in the PTA, the school board, or other organizations.** These groups are already hard at work in the area of violence prevention, including keeping kids off the streets. (If your time is extremely limited, there may be mailing lists and e-mail groups you can participate in.)

- **Advocate for classes** in anger management, resiliency skills, peer mediation, and conflict resolution at your child's school.

- **Support or sponsor a bully-proofing program.** If your child's school isn't part of the very small percentage that already have implemented these programs, volunteer to help start one. (*See Online Resource Directory.*)

- **Participate in determining what, if any, police presence is necessary** on your kids' campus.

- **Support smaller schools.** Our nation's public schools are bursting at the seams, primarily for economic reasons. Many students are not getting the personalized attention they need in and out of the classroom. Smaller schools reduce the risk of kids getting lost and falling through the cracks.

- **Advocate school budgets that ensure sufficient funding** for highly trained teachers, mental health services, education materials, additional school counselors, campus security, and after-school programs and activities to meet the growing demands for identifying and working with students who need help.

- **Get involved in policymaking** regarding weapons on campus.

- **Start a school crime watch program** to monitor corridors, parking lots, and routes to and from school. Student patrols can be an integral part of the program.

10. Get involved in your community.

- **Contact groups focused on violence prevention.** Ask them how you can be of help. It might be something as simple as taking tickets at a fund-raising event, handing out flyers, putting up posters, assisting with transportation, or volunteering to edit the PTA newsletter.

- **Personally support victims of violence.** Victims' assistance programs help victims of violence heal.

- **Set up or volunteer on a violence-prevention hotline.** Make your child aware of telephone numbers and web-sites he or she can use to anonymously report violence or threats. (*See Online Resource Directory for 800-nunber hotline resources.*)

- **Join or support public awareness campaigns.** One school district has initiated a "Pledge to Be Violence-Free." (*See Online Resource Directory for listings of similar campaigns.*)

- **Work with local corporations and the media** to play a positive role in making our schools safer. Call upon their help and generosity in the name of corporate citizenship and community involvement.

- **Involve yourself in a local or national effort to prevent school violence and help victims.** Government-sponsored victim's assistance programs, and grass-roots organizations like Mothers Against Violence in America (MAVIA) are all making a difference. (*See Online Resource Directory for more complete listings.*)

- **Support family, church, and community programs** where kids can "belong" to groups or teams—not gangs—and earn respect.

- **Get involved in determining the laws, policies, and procedures** that keep our children safe. At the very least, write your congressional representative about your concerns.

- **Support gang prevention programs** in your community to ensure safety on the streets. There are too many preventable instances in which kids are the victims of "drive-bys" or other gang violence.

- **Support community organizations** that keep kids off the streets.

- **Support anti-hate campaigns.** Hatred breeds violence. Some of us hate people just because they're different: black, white, Hispanic, Asian, Russian, Arab,gay. Anti-hate campaigns and programs prevent racism and prejudice from growing in our schools and neighborhoods, and in so doing, prevent violence.

- **Support "restorative justice" programs** for kids who get caught committing violent crimes. Prison or youth correction facilities can make kids more violent. Restorative justice programs provide vocational education and job training and teach self-control through anger management, "tough love," and personal responsibility.

Volunteering gives you a chance to lend a hand in helping all kids have healthy outlets. Volunteering is also a way of getting closer to your child.

HEALTHY CONTROVERSY

Parents, school board members, teachers, school administrators, and citizens who voice their opinion about what makes schools safe don't always agree. Or share the same concerns. This controversy is healthy when all parties show respect, listen, and learn from one another and search for common ground. No political grandstanding. No stalemates. No screaming matches. Kids see a powerful example of adults working out their differences, breaking through impasses, and making changes in their best interests.

ACT NOW

The time to act is now. Not after a tragedy happens. We need to sharpen our violence-prevention tools and use them to keep our kids safe. This means knowing where they are, becoming familiar with their friends, setting healthy limits, and staying in touch with what's happening in their ever-widening world. It also means being informed and involved in preventing violence, whether at our children's school or in the community.

Using the tools that you've just read about and developing new tools, are the best ways to keep our children safe—today and tomorrow. In the next chapter we'll learn how they can keep themselves safe.

'0% OF ALL HIGH SCHOOL-AGE BOYS REPORTED THAT THEY WERE IN A PHYSICAL FIGHT ON SCHOOL PROPERTY IN THE

CHAPTER 6

'AST YEAR.—*CDC*[2] ■ 1 IN 7 SCHOOLCHILDREN IS EITHER A BULLY OR A VICTIM, AND 1 IN 5 VICTIMS HAS ACADEMIC

'ROBLEMS BECAUSE OF IT.—*US DOE*[1] ■ A US DOE STUDY SHOWED THAT 25% OF THE SCHOOL BULLIES IT

YOUR

'RACKED HAD CRIMINAL RECORDS BEFORE THEY WERE 30.—*OKIE*[1] ■ 22% OF LARGE CITIES, 25% OF SUBURBAN

CHILD'S

;OUNTIES, 31% OF SMALL CITIES, AND 36% OF RURAL COUNTIES REPORTED THAT THEIR GANG PROBLEM WAS

VIOLENCE-

;ETTING WORSE. —*NYGC* ■ TREATMENT FOCUSED ON ANGER AND STRESS MANAGEMENT, COMMUNICATION

PREVENTION

'ND ASSERTIVENESS SKILLS, FAMILY LIFE, AND SELF-ESTEEM, INCLUDING PARENTAL INVOLVEMENT, PRODUCED

TOOLBOX

;RADUATES MUCH LESS LIKELY TO COMMIT CRIMES IN THE YEAR FOLLOWING TREATMENT THAN YOUTH NOT

N THE PROGRAMS. —*JAACAP* ■ BEHAVIOR MODIFICATION INTERVENTIONS FOCUSING ON CONDUCT, ATTENDANCE,

'ND ACADEMIC ACHIEVEMENT CAN REDUCE SUBSTANCE USE, CRIMINAL ACTIVITY, AND ARRESTS. —*USSG.*[4]

Today we have to address issues with our children that our parents never even thought about. We have to teach our children new ways to get along in a much more dangerous world. In the times when we will not be there to protect them, how will they protect themselves? Equipping them now with violence-prevention survival skills will make all the difference in keeping them safe. The way to cultivate these skills is to provide our children with the right tools. This chapter describes what these essential tools are and how to put them in your child's toolbox.

THE AWARENESS TOOL

Being alert to the forewarnings of violence is one of the most important things children can do to protect themselves. Noticing their surroundings, learning how to "read" people, and recognizing potentially violent situations take time and maturity. With your help, your child will develop her awareness early, get into the habit of paying attention to her surroundings, and avert danger.

Here are some common situations in which your child will need to sharpen her awareness as she gets older:

1. **Around new friends.** As your child enters middle and high school he will be meeting hundreds of kids and making new friends. Some will be good influences, others will put him at risk. Show him the difference. Giving examples, help him see how hanging out with the wrong kids may be putting him in harm's way.

2. **Having new experiences.** As children get older they'll have hundreds of new experiences on their own. They'll visit new parts of town, go to parties where they won't know everyone, begin dating, get their driver's licenses, and ride in cars with their classmates. Most of these new experiences will involve good, clean fun—yet some are bound to involve drugs, drinking and driving, sex and violence. Talk with your child about the risks she may encounter that could ruin a great time. Make clear agreements about each of these risk factors. (See Chapter 3 for how to have these discussions.)

3. **In unfamiliar surroundings.** Children need to be alert to danger. Recognizing when they're in bad neighborhoods, knowing where exits are in a dance club, or when to say, "Stop the car and let me out right here," are all acts of awareness to avert danger. It's always good to arrange dry runs prior to their first rock concert, cross-town sleepover, or out-of-town visit with a cousin. Cell phones (lend them yours) and pagers make "check-ins" easy and can keep you in close touch with your child.

4. **At friends' homes.** When your child visits friends, he should be alert to the "vibe" (the atmosphere) in the house. If the parents are never home, or there's evidence of possible drug use, domestic violence, or guns are accessible, a warning flag should go up. It is essential that your child knows he can call you to come get him anytime, night or day, and talk to you about anything that makes him uncomfortable at a friend's home.

5. **Changes in body language.** The threat of danger can sometimes be detected in body language—if people glare at you, stand too close, slouch in arrogant ways, get "in your face" to talk to you, etc. Teach your child how people send nonverbal "warning signals" when they are angry or scared through body language.

6. **Vocal tone.** The warning signs of violence can be communicated in many ways. Screaming, cursing, and verbal threats are easy to recognize. A low, quiet tone or heavy sarcasm can also mask anger or a threat. If you think your child is missing verbal cues, play-act situations with him and help him learn. Make it a game, but at the same time make sure he knows how important it is to listen between the lines.

> *Reality Check* It's easy to overreact when our children threaten extreme behavior—that is, tell us they want to hurt someone. Stay calm as you sort out whether they really mean it. After venting their anger they'll probably feel a whole lot better and you can breathe a sigh of relief. If your instincts tell you they might do something stupid, stay involved until you're sure they're OK.

THE "JUST SAY NO" TOOL

We hear it everywhere: "Just say no!" But it's not that easy. Kids flirt with danger even when they know it's wrong. They don't think anything bad can happen to them—they're invincible! How can we teach our kids not to take foolish risks and do the right thing, even if their friends are doing the opposite?

Say you overhear your son plotting a potentially dangerous prank to get back at a teacher in school. Some things you can tell him:

- "I know there's a lot of pressure on you to go through with this prank. I need you to say 'no' even though your friends are doing it."

- "You've gotta make the tough choice and say 'no,' even if your friends are already saying 'yes.' Will you agree with me not to do this?"

- "I'm not saying this is easy. But I want you to agree that, no matter what, you will not take part in this prank. Are we agreed?"

Reality Check Parents must also keep alert. Kids need to be made aware of the various kinds of human predators. These people pose a very real threat to kids, especially because they act nice to lure children into their webs before hurting or taking advantage of them. Two ironclad rules, especially for younger kids are: "Always tell Mom or Dad if some new person is being very nice and offers to give you things," and "Always check first with us before going anywhere or agreeing to anything."

THE ANGER-MANAGEMENT TOOL

"Managing" anger—our own and that of others—is a crucial and effective violence-prevention tool. Emotions signal our reactions to internal and external events. Anger is the emotion that tells us we're hurt, frustrated, or disappointed. We need to show our children how to deal with anger constructively so it never turns violent.

WHAT TO SAY ABOUT MANAGING ANGER

- "Anger is normal. It's a natural part of life. We all get angry. But you need to learn how to handle it."

- "Talk about what's making you upset. It will help." Venting anger appropriately releases the pressure building up inside of us. Remember, a child needs a safe harbor with a parent who will listen, not criticize, not become defensive, when he tells you why he's angry. If your child is afraid to talk to you, he won't.

- "If you can't talk to me, maybe you can talk to your father/mother/ brother/sister/school counselor about what's upsetting you."

- "Throwing tantrums may provide momentary relief or give you the feeling you're in control, but they rarely accomplish anything—and may set off an explosion in someone else."

- "Let's talk about what's bothering you and come up with a game plan. If and when this happens again, you'll know what to do."

- "I see how angry you are at your friend. I'd be angry, too. But letting him get the best of you and seeking revenge is only going to make things worse. It isn't worth it."

- "If your friend is angry with you, hear him out. Maybe you guys can talk it out and still be good friends."

- "Occasionally, people see things so differently that working things out isn't possible. If you've tried everything and nothing works, the best thing to do is to agree to disagree and let it go at that."

CONSTRUCTIVE ANGER

Anger can be positive. Constructive confrontations—"having it out"—can clear the air, forge new understanding, and build trust and respect between people who have had serious differences. What differentiates constructive anger from the other kind is that it "takes responsibility." A constructive anger exchange usually begins with "I." This says about you: "I am frustrated, I am hurt, I am disappointed, I am angry. And I want to work things out." Your goal is to identify your part in the dispute and reach a positive outcome—not to grill the other person as if he's on trial. Blaming or accusing anger, on the other hand, does just that. Every sentence begins with "You," as in: "You don't care!" or "You lied to me!" or "It's all YOUR fault!"

Show your kids how to discuss and resolve disputes, including potentially violent ones, without resorting to blame. Here are some examples of how kids can confront kids in constructive ways:

- "I know you're doing the best you can, but I'm still angry with you for being late. How can we work this out?"

- "I thought we agreed on [this problem], but I may be wrong. Let's talk about it."

- "I could have been clearer by asking you not to tell anyone, but when you did I felt betrayed. I told myself you didn't care. I know you really do care, and I don't want to put distance between us."

- "I heard everyone went to the game together the other night, but I was hurt because no one called me. Maybe I'm doing something to turn people off—can you clue me in?"

- "I'm not bringing this up to hurt you or blame you. I just need to get it straight in my own mind. You weren't honest with me and I want to talk about it so I don't stay angry."

- "I think we both dropped the ball. I let things slide, but I believe you didn't follow up, either. Maybe we can talk about what happened and avoid it in the future."

WHEN TO TALK TO YOUR KIDS ABOUT THEIR ANGER

We teach our children from an early age how to get along with others, how to work out their differences peacefully. What happens if their anger is becoming a problem? Or, they throw a tantrum every time they don't get what they want. Or they get into constant fights at school. When is the best time to talk to them about getting their anger under control?

■ In "peacetime." A child is less defensive, more open to listening, and better able to learn in a moment of calm. The middle of an argument may be the worst and most difficult time to reason with him about his anger.

■ Any time your child opens the door. If your child tells you she is angry, or looks upset, ask her what's going on. Listen patiently and find out why she's angry. Then, talk her through what she's doing to deal with her anger, whether it's working, and what her other options are. Remember: keep your questions neutral.

■ After an incident like a fistfight, temper tantrum, or school suspension your child will experience the negative consequences of letting his anger get the best of him. There can be two positive outcomes. First, this opens the door for a valuable life lesson in self-control. Second, it can change the way your child handles anger.

WHAT TO SAY WHEN YOUR CHILD IS EXTREMELY ANGRY

When your child gets very angry, you have a unique opportunity to lend an ear, or a shoulder to cry on, and to help her blow off steam. As she describes the particulars of her situation, listen and allow her to rant about what happened. She's likely to be very hurt, upset, and may even make threatening and radical remarks. Respond with empathy and constructive feedback. Keep her focused on the big picture, which is always safety. Here are some examples:

When your kids say:	YOU should say:
"I won't let him get away with this!" Or, "He'll be sorry he ever messed with me!" Or, "I'm going to make him pay!" Or, "I'm going to kill him!"	"I know how angry you are. I understand you feel he should have to suffer consequences for what he did. Retaliating will only make things worse. Don't you think he'll try to get you back? More violence won't help you resolve the situation; it's only going to continue the cycle. Let's think of some ways to end this."
"It's not fair."	"No, it's not fair. And neither is life sometimes."
"This is it. My life is over." "Things will never be the same again."	"I can see how it feels that way now. One day you may look back at this and think of how far you've come, or even laugh. I know that doesn't offer much comfort now, but try to think ahead to how you might feel different than you're feeling now."
"I can't stand the way I'm being picked on/bullied/made fun of." "I can't go on anymore." "I can't face anyone ever again."	"I can see how humiliated you are, and I might want to crawl into a hole and hide if I went through what you did. Things might be rough for a while, but we're going to figure this out, you'll see."
"I'm not going back to school."	"It *is* a miserable situation, but I think we can do something about it."

When your kids say:	YOU should say:
"You don't know what it's like." Or, "Things are different from when you were growing up." Or, "You don't get it!"	"I know you don't think I understand. And I know things are different from when I was growing up. But I still want you to give what I have to say a chance."
"I feel so dumb." "I feel so lame." "I feel like such a loser."	"I can see why you're upset, but do you think your real friends will think any less of you? You'll see, they'll stand by you."
"Everyone is gonna hate me now, I'm not gonna have any friends."	"Anyone who puts you down or doesn't want to be friends with you as a result of this isn't worth your time."

Your children will get the message: *Problems, even nasty ones, can be handled with restraint, self-control, and patience. There are many ways to do that.*

HEALTHY OUTLETS FOR ANGER

Growing up is a frustrating experience at best. Every kid needs constructive ways to "let it all out." Make sure your child has a variety of healthy outlets for releasing his anger. These may include talking it out with the person he's upset with, going for a walk, working out, journal writing, slugging a punching bag, or making expressive art. Read more about healthy outlets in Chapter 10.

Some kids may need additional help to control their anger. Fortunately, more and more schools and communities now offer anger management classes (*see Online Resource Directory*). If it's going to take more than an anger management class to help your child regain control, consult a mental health professional who specializes in anger control problems.

10 TOOLS TO PROTECT AGAINST BULLIES

Does your child know what to do if confronted by a bully, or any angry, potentially violent individual?

The best strategy is, of course, to avoid the people and situations that put him at risk. But danger cannot always be avoided. Say a known gang member purposely bumps into your son in school. What's the smartest thing he can do? Tell the other kid to "Back off!"? Follow him down the hall and shove him back? Make threatening remarks and tell him he'll meet him after school?

The gang member wants to humiliate your son. Your son has his pride. But what if the gang member has a weapon? Surely your child's life is not worth risking over a bump in the hallway. How can your son avoid a confrontation, or a possible school suspension (now mandatory in many schools for anyone involved in a fight), and maintain his self-respect? What should you advise him to do? Following are ten nonconfrontational strategies your child can use to safely get out of a dangerous situation, safely defend himself—and save his pride.

1. **Stay calm and alert.** When dealing with an extremely angry individual, do nothing that will escalate the situation. Take a deep breath and consider the options. You might say something to diffuse the bully's anger, such as, "I don't want any trouble." The goal is to get out of there, even when this means not acting on what you are burning to say or do.

2. **Just walk away.** Fighting with somebody who's trying to pick a fight with you is not worth it. Especially if the bully is dangerous. Don't allow yourself to be suckered into fighting over nothing. There's nothing to be gained and nothing to prove. Walk away with your shoulders straight and your head held high. Nothing has been lost.

3. **Take it private.** An angry student may feel he has to prove himself and follow through on a threat when his friends are watching. You might say: "Can we go somewhere to talk about this privately?" If the other guy agrees, move the conversation to a safe public location.

4. **Take a nonviolent stand.** Stating your intention not to fight may be the safest thing you can do. Past victims of violence will tell you this is smart, not cowardly. Remember that self-respect comes from the inside, not from proving one's self to the outside world. Things to say that work:

   ■ "I'll talk it out with you, but I'm not going to fight you."

   ■ "I don't want any trouble."

   ■ "Let's both chill out and settle this thing peacefully."

   ■ "I have nothing against you. And nothing to prove. Let's just forget about it."

5. **Report it to the authorities.** Children and their parents often don't report bullying or violence because they're afraid of revenge. In the movies, karate classes turn skinny kids into martial arts machines that beat up the bullies and gain their lifelong respect. In real life, however, when the bully is confronted, he often doesn't go away. He's at school every day, being a bully, until someone reports him. Before filing a bullying complaint, however, discuss with the school and police how they will protect you from retribution (more about staying anonymous in Chapter 9).

6. **Don't make wisecracks.** Making light of the situation, joking nervously, being sarcastic, or demeaning someone won't result in anyone going away laughing. The situation may only get worse.

7. **Treat the other person with respect.** A show of respect might help calm the situation. If it's someone you know, find out if you've said or done something wrong. Things to say that work:

   ■ "I see you are angry. Obviously I've done something to make you upset." Then let the other person respond. Continue if this seems to be working.

   ■ "I owe you an apology. I am sorry for _____."

   ■ "I hope that in time you can forgive me . . . or let me make it up to you."

8. **Agree with the bully.** In the heat of the moment, you're not going to change the bully's mind and make him a better, more enlightened person. Again, the goal is to get out of there safely. Rather than reacting to the insult and fighting back, agree with the bully. Say, "You're right"—then walk away.

9. **Verbally disarm the bully.** Never do anything to provoke a bully. That's the rule. But if you're cornered and there's no other way out, you might try to disarm the bully with a question. Speaking up assertively, but not combatively, there is more of a chance of being seen as a person, rather than an object of scorn or ridicule. Saying something like, "Hey! Why are you doing this to me?" may get the bully to stop and think, buying you some time and consideration.

10. **Walk, run, struggle, fight, but get away.** Escape! Get out of danger as best as you can and find safety. Call for help, yell for help, and send up a signal that somebody else might notice and come to your aid.

Photocopy this section and leave it in your child's room so he can read it again when he needs to. Kids need to keep a bunch of anti-bully strategies in their toolbox, because rarely will one apply to every situation. If the one your child is using isn't working, he needs to be prepared to switch strategies. Any tactic should be abandoned if it's making matters worse.

Reality Check Talking to your child about how to escape danger is difficult at best. Don't be surprised if he responds with "Right. Then I'm really gonna get my butt kicked." As your child gets older, he will have many choices to make. Now you must learn to let your child begin to make his own decisions about the best way to handle situations as they come up. Allow experience also to be your child's teacher.

HOW NOT TO BECOME A VICTIM

1. **Don't look like a victim.** Self-defense experts have taught us that looking or appearing weak and vulnerable invites taunting or worse. Body language can telegraph our expectation that we'll be targeted. Does your child slump, have a shuffling or tentative walk? Is he afraid to make eye contact? Lovingly coach your child to stand up straight, walk with determination, and look people in the eye. This may take some practice.

2. **Don't set yourself up for trouble.** Hurting or provoking others invites a similar response. Don't meet anger with anger. Treat others with respect and chances are they will respect you.

3. **Don't play the fool.** Children who play the class clown, the buffoon, often take on these roles for attention or laughs—and sometimes they do it in an effort to avoid being beaten up. But "playing the fool" is an open invitation for others' aggression, ridicule, taunting, or humiliation. Teach your child that getting a good laugh is one thing, but nobody deserves to be made fun of or to be a target.

4. **Prepare a "game plan" in advance.** If your children feel they might be targets, help them work out a strategy that fits their particular situation.

It's never OK to be harassed, threatened, humiliated, or verbally or physically abused by any individual or group. Being treated as a victim is unacceptable. Tell your children this as many times as necessary.

GETTING ALONG WITH OTHERS

Kindergartners learn the Golden Rule even before the alphabet. But kids and adults often believe, "An eye for an eye . . . " and get into fights.

Conflict is a part of being human and growing up. Learning to live together, avoid unnecessary conflicts, and resolve differences peacefully are things we learn over a lifetime. Conflict resolution skills are power tools for preventing violence.

Here are some do's and don'ts for resolving conflicts:

DON'T:	DO:
Don't let things build up until they boil over.	Manage your anger by venting it appropriately.
Don't say or do anything that provokes violence.	Think before you speak, especially if you're upset or angry.
Don't show disrespect, ridicule, cruelty, or be mean-spirited.	Show respect even if you strongly disagree with or dislike someone.
Don't hate anyone because of their race, religion, ethnicity, or sexuality.	Be tolerant, understanding, and accepting of others.
Don't taunt or make fun of other people, or make life harder for anyone.	Live and let live. Be direct and forthright, but kind.
Don't say you'll do something and not follow through.	Apologize. If you dropped the ball, explain to the person you let down why it happened. Ask forgiveness for hurting or upsetting someone else.
Don't leave any unfinished business. It breeds distrust.	Make time to clear the air.

PARENTHOOD . . . THE ULTIMATE BALANCING ACT

It's our job to strike the balance between protecting our children and letting them go. We want them to learn to use good judgment and to handle themselves in the world. We don't want to see them suffer or fail.

Give your children the tools they need to get along with others. Set reasonable limits on their activities. Don't be overprotective or permissive. When they're ready, give them added responsibilities and freedoms. It isn't easy, but it's our job to prepare our children for our tumultuous—yet wonderful world.

CHAPTER **7**

DREN ARE ARRESTED EVERY DAY FOR VIOENT CRIMES.—*CDF* ■ 28% OF ADOLESCENT BOYS CARRIED A WEAPON—A GUN,

KNIFE, OR CLUB—WITH 13% CARRYING A WEAPON TO SCHOOL IN THE PREVIOUS MONTH.—*CDC*[2] ■ TWO-THIRDS OF U.S.

WHEN

TEENS REPORT THEY CAN GET A GUN IN AN HOUR.—*BORBA*[2] ■ 78% OF PUBLIC SCHOOLS SURVEYED HAVE SOME TYPE

CHILDREN

OF FORMAL SCHOOL VIOLENCE PREVENTION OR REDUCTION PROGRAM—*US DOE*[2] ■ 24% OF HIGH SCHOOL PUPILS SAY

BRING

THEY TOOK A WEAPON TO SCHOOL AT LEAST ONCE IN THE PAST YEAR.—*JIE* ■ 77% OF SCHOOL DEATHS ARE CAUSED BY

WEAPONS

FIREARMS.—*AACAP* ■ OVER 6,000 STUDENTS WERE EXPELLED IN 1996-97 FOR BRINGING GUNS TO SCHOOL.—*AMA*

TO SCHOOL

JUVENILE ARRESTS FOR SERIOUS VIOLENT CRIMES ROSE 67% FROM 1986 TO 1995.—*YMCA*[1] ■ CHILDREN ARE MOST FRE-

QUENTLY INJURED BY FIREARMS WHEN THEY ARE UNSUPERVISED AND OUT OF SCHOOL, USUALLY LATE AFTERNOON,

PEAKING BETWEEN 4 AND 5 P.M., OVER THE WEEKEND, AND DURING SUMMER AND HOLIDAY BREAKS.—*OKIE*[2]

Federal and state laws prohibit kids from bringing weapons on campus. And yet, we know it happens. Children bring guns, knives, and even bombs into schools. Most of us aren't prepared for this. We barely know where to begin the discussion about weapons in school.

This chapter will explain what your child should do if he encounters a weapon in school, what to do if he or she is in immediate danger, and your responsibilities if your child tells you about a weapon.

THREATS: KIDS WHO MAKE THEM AND KIDS WHO RECEIVE THEM

"I'll kill you!" There was a time such words were considered harmless. Not anymore. Today, every threat must be taken seriously. Your child's school should have in place a well-thought-out threat response system, supervised by a threat assessment coordinator and/or team made up of school, mental health, and law enforcement personnel. Response programs provide methods for evaluating threats and policies for responding to them. Other aspects of a threat response program are:

- Procedures for reporting threats from inside and outside the school.

- Guidelines for notifying potential victims and determining what additional legal and security measures, if any, are necessary to protect potential victims after a threat.

- Policies for releasing threat-related information to the school community or media.

- Procedures for filing threat reports with school and law enforcement representatives who will monitor and prevent potential acts of violence.

- Policies for counseling and monitoring the threat-makers to make sure they are not a danger to themselves or others in the future.

Threats cannot be ignored. You must determine whether a threat is real— and at the same time not treat every incident as a major danger. School and law enforcement experts can walk you through the process of how to assess and deal with a threat.

Effective threat response can deter future threats. Students think twice if they know threats will be reported, investigated, and dealt with firmly. A strong response to a threat also sends the message to the school community that a system is in place to ensure their safety.

IF YOUR CHILD ENCOUNTERS WEAPONS IN SCHOOL

If your child tells you he knows or suspects that one or more students are bringing weapons into his school or issuing threats, or if he actually sees a weapon in someone's jacket, locker, or backpack, what should he do?

DON'T:	DO:
Don't do anything to put yourself in danger, such as taking matters into your own hands.	Go to a phone or to someone in authority ASAP. Be specific and report the details.
Don't go around telling your friends. Word may get back to the person carrying the weapon that you have been talking about him.	Talk about it only to the authorities. They will know how to handle the situation.
Don't ignore, minimize, or deny the danger of someone having a weapon. "It's OK, he's not going to hurt anyone," is a cop-out.	Take responsibility for making your school and neighborhood safer by taking safe action.
Don't antagonize the person carrying the weapon, or try to take it away from him.	Try to calm down and reason with the person carrying the weapon, especially if there's no escape and you or another are at risk.
Don't, if you come across a weapon, touch it, but don't leave it unattended.	If you see or discover an unattended weapon, send someone for help.

IF YOUR CHILD MUST ESCAPE A DANGEROUS SITUATION:

If violence ever breaks out on your child's campus, she must know self-defense and escape strategies. These tactics are best taught by skilled professionals in a classroom setting. Children learn nonconfrontational approaches and escape techniques, including how to think on their feet about the strategy that best fits their situation.

The basics of self-protection:

- **Don't hesitate,** panic, or do anything to draw attention to yourself.

- **Get yourself out of there.** Help others get away.

- **If someone is in immediate and imminent danger,** warn with, "Get out of here! He's got a gun!" But don't get hysterical—it might just inflame the situation.

- **Don't turn your back on others** who may also be in danger.

- **Don't go over to see what's happening** if you suspect someone has fired a shot (a real gunshot sounds more like a firecracker than movie gunshots).

- **Run for cover** away from where the shots are coming from.

Many martial arts studios now also teach kids how to defend themselves and escape from school violence. (*See Online Resource Directory for a listing of books on self-defense strategies and school-based programs.*)

IF YOUR CHILD TELLS YOU ABOUT A WEAPON:

1. **Take immediate action.** Time is of the essence. Contact the school and police department immediately and report that a weapon has been seen on campus.

2. **Have your facts straight** so that the situation can be properly reported and investigated. You can request that your child's identity remain anonymous (see rule #7).

3. **Praise your child's courage and character.** Thank him for coming to you and calmly discuss a plan of action. Even though you might be frightened, do not panic or overreact.

4. **Include your child in the planning and reporting process** so he will know how to handle situations like this in the future.

5. **Reassure your child.** He or she is doing the right thing by going to the authorities. Doing the right thing is not always going to be easy.

6. **Let your child see you acting calm and respectful** in your dealings with the school or investigating police officer.

7. **Determine how school and law enforcement officials will protect** your child's anonymity and keep him safe from retribution. With your child present, make clear agreements about precisely how this will be done. Assure him that nothing you are planning to do will put him at risk.

8. **Get a timeline for action to be taken.** Ask, "How and when will we know that this has been taken care of?"

9. **Be politely persistent** until you are satisfied the situation will be handled safely and in accordance with the law.

10. If reporting the incident does not yield satisfactory results, go a step higher. In rare instances, first reports aren't enough to get results. In these cases, it's appropriate to go directly to the chief of police, the superintendent of schools, or the State Department of Education. If repeated attempts to get school or law enforcement officials to respond to a threat or act of violence has not resulted in appropriate action, you may want to file a formal complaint. This should be considered only in extreme cases.

11. Follow up. Call your local police department to verify that the incident was handled. Show your gratitude by thanking the officers who helped you.

12. Be an advocate, not an adversary. Work with your child's school and the police department, not against them. Show respect. Find the balance between being assertive and demanding.

THE PARENT/SCHOOL/COMMUNITY SAFETY CONNECTION

The awful reality is that keeping our schools weapons-free is an ongoing challenge for parents, school, and law enforcement. Fortunately, good laws that protect our children have been enacted. The federal Gun-Free Schools Act of 1994 requires schools to report incidents of any child who carries a weapon. But this and other laws are not always easy to enforce.

Here are four ways you can work with your child's school and the local police to prevent violence and keep schools weapons-free.

1. Volunteer your time at your child's school or local law enforcement agency as a safety volunteer.

2. Become a safety watchdog. Parents can join with others to follow up on weapons incidents and make sure effective action is being taken by the school, law enforcement, courts, legislators, and the offender's parents. Parent watchdogs ensure accountability and action.

3. **Make reporting easier for our children.** Children are the eyes and ears of their school. They know just about everything that is happening. But will they tell? Studies indicate that 50 percent would not report a classmate with a weapon on campus. This reluctance is partly based on their fear of getting into trouble and, worse, that reporting the incident will not make a difference. This is sad—and unacceptable!

School hotlines, classroom training programs for students, teachers, and staff, and on-site school security officers—an atmosphere of violence-prevention awareness—all make it easier for kids to report weapons, threats, or well-founded suspicions to the proper authorities. (*For more on these violence-prevention programs and resources, see Chapter 10 and the Online Resource Directory.*)

4. **Become a safety advocate.** Our legal system and our laws are not perfect, nor are the people in charge of enforcing them. Sometimes it takes time, hard work, and partnering with the authorities to improve upon the law. Recall for a moment the evolution of automobile seat belt laws. For too many years state regulations were lax about enforcing these laws, despite knowing that seat belts saved lives. Now these laws are enforced nationwide, leading to a dramatic decline in automobile fatalities and injuries. In the same spirit, we need to insist that laws against bringing weapons to school get enforced before more children are killed or injured.

There may be parent advocate groups in your community who share your concerns. Or you may be one of the few—and brave—parents to stand up and speak out about the need for better safety policies and practices. Here are ways you can become a safety advocate:

- Join or start a safety advocacy group. Seek out one that addresses your specific concerns.

- Call your congressional representative. Get attention for your concerns and possibly move along proposed laws that will better protect our kids.

- Make sure the schools and police have the necessary training, money and resources to do their job and make your child's school safer.

- Donate money to a nonprofit organization that is helping to make schools safer.

HAVE THE "WEAPONS TALK"

Weapons have no place on a school campus. In addition to being illegal, they are an invitation to disaster. This chapter has equipped you to have the "weapons talk" with your child right now. Put it at the top of your To Do list. Talk to your child in detail about what to do if someone brings a weapon to school, how to escape, and where to go for help.

We need to make it easier and safer for kids to report weapons. We need better weapons laws and policies for our schools, and the power to enforce them. As parents we have the most to lose, and the most to gain by being informed and involved.

Reality Check Extremely serious matters like threats of violence, guns, laws, and even jail time are tough to handle. If your child has been threatened, or has made threats, this is the time he needs you the most. You're probably scared. And so is your child. Take a deep breath. Take your child by the hand. Get involved—this is serious business requiring a serious response. Be strong! And take pride in being a role model for character strength and courage.

A CHILD WHO SPENDS 13 YEARS IN AVERAGE PUBLIC SCHOOLS HAS 1 CHANCE IN 107,000 OF A VIOLENT DEATH.—*YWCA*[1]

CHAPTER **8**

81% OF SCHOOL DEATHS ARE HOMICIDES.—*YWCA*[1] ■ THE HOMICIDE RATE IS NINE TIMES HIGHER IN URBAN SCHOOLS

THAN IN RURAL ONES. 83% OF VICTIMS AND 96% OF KILLERS ARE MALE.—*YWCA*[1] ■ SINCE WORLD WAR II, THERE

IF

HAS BEEN A SEVENFOLD INCREASE IN SERIOUS ASSAULT BY JUVENILES IN THE UNITED STATES.—*US DOJ* ■ 52% OF

VIOLENCE

AMERICAN TEENS THINK THEIR SCHOOL COULD BE STRUCK BY THE KIND OF MASSACRE THAT DEVASTATED

HAPPENS

COLUMBINE HIGH SCHOOL.—*NYT/CBS* ■ 43% OF STUDENTS DO NOT FEEL SAFE USING THE SCHOOL

RESTROOMS.—*APA* ■ 4.0% OF HIGH SCHOOL STUDENTS NATIONWIDE MISSED ONE OR MORE DAYS OF SCHOOL IN THE

PAST MONTH BECAUSE THEY FELT UNSAFE TRAVELING TO OR FROM SCHOOL.—*US DOE*[1] ■ ADOLESCENT VIOLENCE

IN GENERAL AND HOMICIDE IN PARTICULAR HAS DECREASED SINCE 1993.—*FBI*[3] ■ VIOLENT BEHAVIOR DEVELOPS

PROGRESSIVELY AND THERE ARE OBSERVABLE SIGNS ALONG THE WAY IF WE KNOW WHAT TO LOOK FOR. —*FBI*[3]

None of us wants to consider the possibility that violence could happen in our child's school. It is simply too horrifying to imagine. But the fact is, what happened at Columbine, Santana, and twenty-five other American schools can happen anywhere.

What if the unthinkable happened? Are our children's schools prepared? Are we prepared?

ARE OUR CHILDREN'S SCHOOLS PREPARED?

Most districts now require each school to have in place comprehensive policies and emergency procedures that address and deal with school violence. The safety policies and emergency plans listed below should be in effect in your child's school.

SCHOOL VIOLENCE-PREVENTION POLICIES

1. **Strict adherence to weapons laws.**

2. **Strict disciplinary action for threats of violence.**

3. **Mandatory evaluation and counseling** for any child showing signs of violent or self-destructive behavior.

4. **Staff training** in violence prevention and emergency response, including initial trauma counseling for victims.

5. **Safety drills** to prepare students and teachers for the possibility of violence on campus.

SCHOOL VIOLENCE-INTERVENTION PROCEDURES

1. **A fully detailed disaster plan** for how to immediately respond to an incident of violence including lockdown and evacuation procedures, and a multi-signal alarm system.

2. **A coordinated emergency response team** that involves the local police and fire departments and medical emergency team.

3. **Crisis counseling** for victims suffering physical and emotional trauma.

4. **Backup emergency communications** ready to function if normal in-school phone communications are interrupted.

5. **An up-to-date database of parents and parent alternates** to contact and to whom students can be released in the event of a school emergency.

The best school emergency plans are those that constantly improve and get better, simpler, and easier to follow. If you think there is something more your child's school could be doing to handle an incident of violence, or to prevent one, suggest it!

ARE OUR CHILDREN PREPARED?

How much do your kids know about their school's safety practices? Sit down with them and calmly do a step-by-step review. "Scare tactics" can have an extremely adverse effect on children, especially the younger ones.

Knowing the answers to these questions will help your child feel more secure and prepared:

- "Do you know how to report weapons on campus or a threat of violence?"

- "Have you taken part in safety drills in which an act of violence was staged?"

- "Do you know how to protect yourself if violence happens?"

- "What is your school's crisis communication or signaling system?" (Such as: steady ring = Get Out; on/off ring = Stay Where You Are.)

- "Do you know all the ways to communicate in the middle of an incident?" (Pay phones, emergency phones, cell phones, alarms, etc.)

- "Do you know who will be in charge if violence occurs at your school?"

- "Do you know what to do to survive if someone has a gun, a bomb, a knife, or other weapon and is threatening others?"

IF VIOLENCE HAPPENS, WHAT TO EXPECT

The following general sequence of emergency response procedures is based on the experience and expertise of several large school districts.

1. **An alert witness or victim calls for help.** The student may call 911, yell for help, or run to a school security officer. If the student calls the police, a dispatcher will ask questions and order an emergency response.

2. **School personnel implement their "school disaster plan,"** performing in their assigned roles.

3. **"Lockdown" and/or evacuation may occur.** Upon notification of danger at or near the school, an emergency signal directs teachers and kids to secure their classrooms (lockdown) or evacuate. In lockdown, doors and windows are locked, blinds drawn, and children are told to "stay down until all is clear." Students not in class are instructed to seek safe shelter until the police arrive and they are given further instructions. If the signal is to evacuate, children are directed to leave the campus in an orderly manner.

4. **Police arrive and take charge.** The violence is contained, the perpetrator(s) are apprehended, and weapons are confiscated. Police and trauma units seal off the crime scene.

5. **Emergency medical care is given.** Those injured or in need are administered to and transported to local hospitals if necessary.

6. **The criminal investigation begins.** The police or FBI unit will detain children, teachers, or other witnesses at the school or at a nearby site to interview them and reconstruct the sequence of events.

7. **Trauma intervention begins.** Crisis counselors from the police and mental health community offer comfort and counseling. Parents are notified, brought to a holding area, debriefed about what has occurred, and coached about how to help their traumatized child.

8. **Information sharing.** A school or police spokesperson briefs students, parents, teachers, and the media about what has happened. The status of victims and others involved in the incident is reported.

Reality Check You're very upset. When you asked your daughter where she'd go and what she'd do in case of a school emergency, she didn't have a clue. You think to yourself, "Why didn't she learn this in school??!!" Don't lose it. Call the school, make an appointment with the counselor or principal, and ask how you can work together to make sure your child and all the other students know what to do in case of an emergency. Balance patience with persistence.

THE THREE PHASES OF COPING

Children who are closest to the epicenter of an act of school violence, or are deeply shocked and disturbed by an incident in another community, are likely to experience shock and trauma. To help them, we need to understand what they are likely to be going through. Having experienced several school shootings firsthand, I observed that children go through three phases:

Phase 1: Shock and disbelief

Phase 2: Reality sets in

Phase 3: Coming to terms

PHASE 1—SHOCK AND DISBELIEF

At first, children go into a natural, protective state of shock. They were invincible one moment and shattered the next. It's difficult to completely accept that someone they know has died or been wounded. Or that this actually happened to them.

The students I met with in the immediate aftermath of the Santana High School shootings expressed the full range of emotions:

- **Outrage** that there had been a shooting at their school involving kids they knew.

- **Disbelief** that someone has been shot or actually died.

- **Overwhelming sorrow** for the students who had been shot, and their families.

- **A need to publicly memorialize** the kids who died. With the help of a local funeral home, they erected a beautiful shrine of flowers, candles, cards, pictures, signs, and teddy bears at the entrance to the school.

- **Intense anger, rage, and disgust** directed toward the shooter.

- **Extreme concern** for their friends who had been wounded or had a "close call."

- **Fear.** Terrified to return to school or even to go home; no place felt safe.

- **Helplessness,** and a desire to turn back the clock to a time to when their lives were normal.

- **Disturbing confusion,** as they asked, "How could someone have done this?"

- **Guilt.** They survived the shootings and wondered, "Why them and not me?" Those who knew the shooter had been threatening violence felt they could have prevented the incident. (This is explored in more detail in Chapter 10.)

In this first phase, every kind of reaction can be expected from our children. Some kids take it very hard; they are completely devastated, unusually quiet, and can't open up to anyone about what happened. Talking about it is simply too difficult or upsetting. Others frantically run around asking questions, or need to tell and retell, step by step, their stories of what happened. Still others seem to be detached from the incident and are in a rush to get on with life as usual. Despite outward appearances, you can be sure they too are all still hurting.

PHASE 2—REALITY SETS IN

In time, the reality of what has happened begins to set in. Those most deeply affected by the violence find themselves in a place of inescapable pain. As others are beginning to move on, they have to accept that their brother, sister, classmate, or best friend is not coming home. Or that their injured dear ones are going to take a long time to heal. These kids are going to need a lot of support. The school can respond to their pain in the following ways:

- Provide continued opportunities for students (and teachers and other school personnel, such as custodial staff) to talk about what happened and how it is affecting them. Support groups and grief counseling are made readily available.

- Hold town hall meetings and school assemblies to honor the deceased. Discuss how to make the school and community safer.

- Parents, teachers, administrators, and organizations mobilize and take concrete action to prevent further incidents (sadly, the period following a crisis is often the only time we enact change). Awareness about violence prevention is heightened.

- Implement safety improvements and strictly enforce safety laws.

- Offer practical and financial assistance to school and community organizations as they reach out to the families of the deceased and injured and provide whatever help is necessary.

PHASE 3—COMING TO TERMS

In the months and years following an act of school violence, children develop some capacity for understanding that tragic events like these happen—in our schools, in our lives. Sometimes they happen to the people we love. Most kids find healthy ways to express their grief, sorrow, and sense of outrage. Some don't, and those kids have an extremely difficult time. What can you do to help your child constructively channel their feelings of grief and come to terms?

- Allow them to grieve. They will need your support.

- If children are experiencing symptoms of post-traumatic stress, such as persisting fear, anxiety, and flashbacks, they will probably benefit from trauma counseling.

- Don't ever rush them. Healing takes as long as it's going to take. There are no set rules in grief. No one knows if it should take a child six weeks, six months, or two years to pass through a phase. In my experience, a child who has witnessed a violent death will probably be dealing with it intensely for several years.

- If your child had a close relationship with the person or persons who died or who committed the act of violence, extra time and help may be needed in sorting through his or her feelings (more about this in the next chapter).

- Some children will be so deeply affected by the loss that it will stay with them over a lifetime. Help them explore ways they might do something good in the world as an "honoring," or expression of love for their friend or fellow student. This may include starting an annual scholarship in the victim's name, getting a new safety law enacted, becoming a peer counselor at school, or even making a career choice such as a school counselor or police officer.

WHAT SHOULD PARENTS DO TO COPE?

Every one of us has experienced, if only for a microsecond, the terror of losing our child—the close call of your child running into the street at age five; the news report of a fatal car accident near his favorite hangout. How are we to react when every parent's nightmare hits close to home? What should we do if one of our child's friends or classmates is killed? Here are ways for us to cope during this traumatic time:

- **Let yourself grieve.** Parents who allow themselves to grieve over the death of their child's friend or classmate are in the best position to help their own child. As you come to terms with the tragedy—that it has happened, that it is real—you'll be better able to listen and talk to your child. In your rush to take care of your child, do not overlook your own shock and grief.

- **Recognize your own sense of helplessness and discomfort.** You can't take away the pain—yours or your child's.

- **Be patient.** Healing takes a long time and each phase of grieving brings its own challenges.

- **Don't feel you need to do this alone.** Get all the help and advice you need.

- **Show your humanity.** By allowing your child to see you grieve, you set a powerful example. By being real, you are saying, "It's OK to feel what you feel—to be sad and cry, to share your feelings with others, to talk about the person who died, to want to remember the person who died by doing something in his or her name."

BE THERE FOR YOUR CHILD

After an incident of violence—whether it has occurred at their school or in another community—your children will need you to be available, physically and emotionally, to help them. Some suggestions:

DON'T:

Don't try to artificially restore a sense of safety or normalcy by giving assurances you can't guarantee.

Don't make it about you or how you would have handled the situation. It's about your child and what she's going through.

Don't avoid or ignore your child's distress or turn off the TV because you're personally uncomfortable. Limit his exposure to graphic news coverage, but don't try to hide what happened.

Don't demonize the perpetrator(s). Concentrating too much attention on the perpetrator distracts from your child's immediate need for understanding and reassurance that she is now safe.

Don't overindulge your child in an effort to help him get through what he's dealing with.

DO:

Create a calm environment for honest, open discussion about any aspect of what happened. Be available . . . always.

Be patient. Let your child know you're with her over the long term. Kids need a parent in control who is a source of strength.

Share any information you've learned that will help your child understand. Help your child think through and begin to construct his own answers. Watch television together in limited doses and talk about it.

Help your child understand how desperate and/or disturbed the perpetrator(s) must have been to have reached the point where they believed violence was their only recourse.

Try to keep a normal routine with meals, bedtime, and the usual school schedule and family activities.

DON'T:

Don't try to "fix" or solve how she feels, as if her feelings themselves were a problem. Don't play the expert.

Don't discuss retribution. You may be blowing off steam, but it sends the wrong message to your kids: that violence is an answer. It may also scare them.

Don't overreact if your child becomes extremely irritable and angry for some time.

Don't crowd your child. Give him "space" and accept that he may need to be with his friends now, not you.

Don't jump in and exploit the tragedy to advance your own agenda, to air a gripe against the school or a school official, or to express a social or political opinion.

DO:

Help her understand that her trauma and loss, like any injury, will take time to heal. Encourage her to take whatever positive steps are necessary, including some form of trauma counseling or a grief support group.

Show respect for those who have died or been injured, for their families, and for others who have been traumatized. Let them see you venting anger constructively.

Hold her and touch her often. Spend extra time with her at bedtime. Remember, you're probably the safest person in whom she can entrust her anger, hurt, fear, and confusion.

Help your child express himself by drawing pictures, writing cards to the surviving families, or attending a religious service.

Support your child's school in its efforts to counsel the students and honor the victims. Speak out against violence and do your part to prevent further violence when the time is right.

PAY YOUR RESPECTS

One important contribution we can make in the wake of a fatal school shooting or incident of violence is to show respect for and support the victims' families. Whether or not we knew them personally, there are many ways to honor the children who died or were wounded and their families. Some honorings are best done in private, behind the scenes, and some are public. In the aftermath of recent national tragedies we witnessed the many ways people publicly expressed their love, prayers, and condolences, including beautiful flower displays, candles, notes, cards, and drawings sent from around the world.

Our children will usually decide by themselves how to pay their respects. If they do ask for help, you might suggest the following:

- Write a personal note to the victim's family, class, or school.

- Attend a memorial service. Speak at the "open mic" and offer a testimonial about how that friend touched you.

- Plant a memorial tree or light a memorial candle at school.

- Visit and/or bring a food basket and flowers to the victim's home.

- Volunteer to help out the family by taking over some household task.

- With the family's permission, help establish an award, a memorial, or an annual event in the victim's name.

Children who escape incidents with severe wounds or trauma must also be remembered, as must their families. Expressions of support may range from "Thinking of You" cards to helping out with medical expenses.

RESPECT THE FAMILY'S PRIVACY

Some grief-stricken or traumatized families prefer to remain private. Call to ask if and when they are receiving visitors, and if so, do not overstay your welcome. They've doubtless received nonstop phone calls and visits, so be extra-sensitive and respectful at this time when they're just struggling to get through the day.

Many people come forward after a tragedy for the right reasons—to express their love, sorrow, and compassion. But tragedies also attract some people for the wrong reasons, such as a morbid sense of curiosity. After a highway accident, traffic gets backed up on both sides of the road when "rubbernecking" drivers slow down to see the wreck. People drive miles just to stand a few yards from the site of a school shooting or terrorist attack. Between too many spectators and the media, scenes of tragedy can take on a feeling of disrespect, chaos, and sensationalism.

HANDLING THE PRESS AND ONLOOKERS

Grieving families are completely vulnerable in the time surrounding their children's death. Knowing this, a family member, neighbor, or close friend usually acts as the go-between. This person's primary function is to help the family screen out people who are there for the wrong reasons. Go-betweens also help the family think out loud and decide how to best take care of themselves. If the death of their loved one has become public and they are being besieged by TV reporters and cameras, it's good to remind the family:

- They do not have to speak to the media if they don't want to.

- If they do agree to be interviewed, they don't need to answer any questions they don't want to answer.

- They need to do things at their own pace and not feel pressured to do anything beyond that.

Individuals close to the family, which may include you or your child, may also be approached for an interview. Assess whether it is a good idea to give an interview, especially right after the incident, when those who have been most deeply hurt are vulnerable and all the facts may not yet be in.

The media can play either an extremely constructive or destructive role in covering a school tragedy. Sometimes parents and school officials need to remind (or inform) reporters that they can make a positive contribution by honoring and memorializing the children who have died or been injured instead of sensationalizing the tragedy. Sensationalizing a child's death and exploiting a family's anguish are unacceptable, no matter how high it might drive the ratings.

AFTER THE CAMERAS ARE GONE

After the wave of media attention is over, the family is left alone to face the harsh reality that they have lost a child or have a wounded child. Staying in touch in the months, even years, following a tragedy is even more critical in showing a family you care. Lighting an anniversary candle or doing something to honor your child's friend's memory assures the family that their son or daughter has not been forgotten. As time goes on they are probably still feeling uncomfortable telling others that they're still grieving. This is when an understanding friend and fellow parent is a godsend.

Reality Check There are some things we just can't fix. Much as you'd like to take away your child's pain and make everything right, you can't. If your child has been handed a painful dose of reality she will have to come to terms with it. Grief and loss are part of growing up and a child must learn how to cope with these feelings. Your role is "being there" for your child. This might mean listening, nothing more. To be silent is not a failure on your part.

CHAPTER 9

BULLYING WAS A FACTOR IN MANY OF THE INCIDENTS.—*GCU* ■ TWO-THIRDS OF THE 41 YOUTHS INVOLVED IN

SCHOOL SHOOTINGS SINCE 1974 SAID THEY HAD BEEN BULLIED AT SCHOOL AND THAT REVENGE WAS ONE OF THEIR

TALKING

MOTIVES.—*USSS* ■ THE AVERAGE CHILD SEES 200,000 VIOLENT ACTS ON TELEVISION (INCLUDING 40,000 MURDERS)

TO YOUR

BY HIGH SCHOOL GRADUATION.—*NIMF* ■ AT AGE 18, YOUTHS WHO FULLY PARTICIPATED IN THE SEATTLE SOCIAL

KIDS

DEVELOPMENT PROJECT HAD LOWER RATES OF VIOLENCE, HEAVY DRINKING, DRUG ABUSE AND SEXUAL ACTIVITY

ABOUT

(INCLUDING MULTIPLE SEXUAL PARTNERS AND PREGNANCY) AND BETTER ACADEMIC PERFORMANCE THAN OTHERS NOT

SCHOOL

IN THE PROGRAM.—*USSG*[1] ■ THE BEHAVIORAL APPROACHES SHOWN TO BE EFFECTIVE IN PREVENTING YOUTH VIOLENCE

VIOLENCE

ARE GENERALLY SCHOOL-BASED AND INCLUDE BEHAVIOR MONITORING AND REINFORCEMENT OF ATTENDANCE, ACA-

DEMIC PROGRESS AND SCHOOL BEHAVIOR, AND BEHAVIORAL TECHNIQUES FOR CLASSROOM MANAGEMENT. —*USSG*[1]

A simple act of violence can shatter a life. A family. A community. A nation.

We're never quite the same. After an act of violence, how can we, as parents, be there for our kids when they've been traumatized or are grieving? How can we help them reconstruct a sense of safety and normalcy? This chapter provides a road map for guiding your children through the dark days of trauma and loss and helping them return to school and the business of growing up.

WHEN VIOLENCE STRIKES ELSEWHERE

The images of students running for their lives after an incident of school violence has become a horrifyingly familiar image on the nightly news. Children may be traumatized by an act of violence they see on TV or read about in the newspaper. It may have occurred on the other side of the country, but the impact is still devastating. If you know or even suspect that your child is upset by violence that occurred somewhere else, try these ways to help:

- Tell her, "It's normal to feel scared and sad or angry when horrible things like this happen . . . either far away, or close to home."

- Ask, "Are you afraid the same thing could happen here?" Ask her to explain.

- Tell him, "I plan to do everything in my power to protect you and make sure something like this will never happen in your school. I will do this by participating in the school and community violence-prevention programs."

- Assure her, "I wouldn't let you go to school unless I felt it was safe. Let me tell you why I think it's safe." Explain what's being done at her school and reassure her of the measures that have been taken to make it unlikely this could happen there.

- Help your child think out loud about the incident by asking, "Tell me what you heard about what happened. How did you find out? How is it affecting you?"

- Assure him, "Sometimes these kinds of feelings last a while. That's OK."

- Assure her, "It may take a while for you to feel better."

- Check back with him by asking, "I know that you were feeling sad about what happened last week. Are you feeling any different now? Tell me how."

- Ask open-ended questions such as, "Why do you think some kids hurt other kids?" And, "What can parents and kids do so that things like this don't happen again?" Let your child's responses and questions lead the discussion.

WHEN VIOLENCE HITS HOME

If there was an incident of violence in your child's school or in your community involving people he knew, your child will probably be experiencing intense sadness, anger, fear—and guilt. Guilt arises when kids feel responsible for the death of a friend or classmate, for a variety of reasons:

- Perhaps his last contact or conversation with the person who was shot or wounded was a negative one.

- Perhaps he feels he could have done something to prevent what happened (most school shooters tell friends what they're planning).

- Perhaps he's asking, "Why them and not me?" This is often referred to as "survivor's guilt."

Reality Check Talking in very real terms about school violence is terribly difficult—for our children and for us. Don't think this is going to be easy. It isn't! If your child is scared or having nightmares about people getting shot, do your best to reassure him. Explain that "these things do happen, but they're not likely to happen at your school." If your child's fears persist, it's not because you haven't done your job. Consult an expert for help.

Children need to be able to struggle and figure out for themselves how and why this incident of violence happened, whether they were in some way responsible, and what could have been done to prevent it. They need to be able to say how they feel—without us making excuses for them or in some way exempting them from the situation.

Make yourself available. Let your child talk. Let him get out his guilt and regrets, which often take the form of what we call "if only's":

- "If only I had told someone."

- "If only I had been nicer to her."

- "If only I had been there."

- "If only I hadn't broken up with him."

Show your child empathy. After listening to the "if only's," reassure him to relieve his guilt:

- "I know how much you cared about _____ [the friend who was hurt or killed]."

- "I know you would have done anything to prevent this from happening."

- "You were a wonderful friend to_____. I can see how much you loved him."

- "Everything you're feeling is so understandable. I'm sure I'd feel the same."

- "I'm so proud of you for being able to talk about this."

- "It sounds like you're blaming yourself for what happened. Is that fair?"

- "Is there something you wish you had done differently in your friendship? Tell me about it."

Once your child has vented his guilt, look him in the eyes and tell him:

- "I don't know why these things happen. I'm so sorry."

- "Is there something you can do in honor of _____ to prevent this from ever happening again?"

- "I know you are blaming yourself. But you couldn't have changed what happened. There was nothing you could have done!" (if this is appropriate).

Our understanding, acceptance, and reassurance are important parts of our child's healing. Here are some suggestions to guide your discussions after an incident of school violence:

DON'T:

Don't panic. Your child is already upset. Avoid saying or doing anything that will make him even more scared.

Don't expect you'll have all the answers. As always, the best way to talk is to listen first. Try to understand what your child is going through.

Don't present yourself as the all-knowing parent with a "quick fix." Avoid oversimplified answers or explanations.

DO:

Be up front with your child. Address his questions and concerns truthfully but sensitively. This way he'll learn to trust you.

Be a sounding board. Allow your child to ask unanswerable questions. More than answers, she needs to struggle with the "whys" that accompany tragedies.

Learn and understand all the facts before you make judgments about what has happened.

DON'T:

Don't make blanket assurances like, "This will never happen again." Kids don't buy it.

Don't show too much enthusiasm when your child first tells you he's feeling better. It may send the wrong message—that his suffering has been a burden to us and we're glad he's finally getting over it.

Don't say, "You shouldn't worry because it happened somewhere else." If he tells you he feels frightened and he is criticized or belittled, he won't bring it up again.

DO:

Talk about the incident and about the school. Discuss the school's current disaster plan and ways to improve on it. Make it clear that you will work to make his school a safer place.

Provide your child with opportunities to grieve and express his emotions for as long as necessary. Be positive without being pushy.

Send the message that it's OK to feel the way he feels. Tell him feeling frightened, angry and sad are normal reactions.

For age-specific suggestions about what to say and do after an incident of school violence see the Online Resource Directory.

WHEN PARENTS BLAME THEMSELVES

Mothers and fathers often blame themselves for the deaths of their children (so do brothers and sisters). In responding to these self-blaming parents, I use the example of my loss. I tell them, "I sent my daughter Jenna on a study-abroad program. She was killed in a bus accident. I should never have let her go. I sent my daughter to her death!"

I then ask parents if they feel I was responsible. Their response is always, "No, Ken, you only wanted the best for your daughter. You sent Jenna around the world thinking it would be the adventure of a lifetime. You couldn't have known this was going to happen."

It's difficult to disarm parents of their guilt, their sense of failure and responsibility, when injuries or deaths of their children are involved. Sometimes trying to talk parents out of their guilt only makes things worse. They blame themselves even more. Parents need to be allowed to express their guilt in order to get to the deep sorrow and yearnings residing just beneath it. They also need to be able to express their anger. In time, we all discover that we're not in control.

We don't have the power to save our children from a deadly disease, a horrible accident, a bullet, or a bomb. We are only human, after all. We can only do so much. We want the best for our children. We would give our lives for them. But sometimes children get hurt and children die. It's not fair. It's a travesty of nature for a parent to outlive their child. But that's the way it is, and no amount of self-blame is going to change this harsh reality.

Reality Check Parents need each other's support, especially during the tough times. It's not like we've done this a hundred times. Words of understanding and reassurance from a husband, wife, another parent, or friend have been known to cure even the most stubborn case of the "I'm a terrible parent" blues. Talking with other adults and exchanging ideas also helps parents talk to their own children.

HOW MUCH INFORMATION DOES A CHILD NEED?

In the weeks following an incident of school violence, some children (and parents as well) are hungry to find out as much as they can about what happened. They crave information to fill in pieces of the puzzle, to help them achieve some understanding of how this could have happened. The more these kids can find out, the more pieces of the puzzle they can put in place. These children seek understanding because that is what helps them, not escape or denial. Their intense appetite for information need not be a cause for concern, unless it becomes an obsession or preoccupation.

On the other hand, children who are already completely overwhelmed by what's happened need to take a break. They've experienced about as much as they can deal with and probably need time off from dealing with "the tragic incident." A temporary escape to the local mountains, river, or ocean might do them a world of good. If they need more than a breather, consult their school about resources to help them cope with the overwhelming feelings they are experiencing.

SHOULD I FORCE MY CHILD TO TALK?

We all have our own timetable for grieving and healing. Some children heal relatively quickly on their own. Some kids go right back to familiar routines such as watching violent movies or playing shoot-'em-up video games. It may seem insensitive, but it's their way of coping. Most children will open up to us in their own time and way when they're ready. Trying to force your child to express his emotions can be counterproductive.

But what if your child doesn't want to talk? What if he snaps, "I'm fine!" every time you ask how he's doing? What if he's spending all of his time with his friends? Should you force him to stay home and talk?

It's natural for kids to seek refuge with their friends after a tragedy. Some degree of denial and avoidance are also natural, but in the long term it doesn't provide relief. Children who completely avoid dealing with any of their feelings can become depressed, act out, or show signs of post-traumatic stress.

SIGNS OF POST-TRAUMATIC STRESS

- Skips school.

- Withdraws from his friends or family.

- Begins drinking or using drugs.

- Has trouble concentrating.

- Loses interest in things he used to like.

- Has flashbacks or nightmares.

- Was previously confident but is now afraid of going back to school.

IF YOUR CHILD WON'T TALK ABOUT IT

1. **Get professional advice.** Call your child's principal, a school counselor, a trusted professional, or your local police department, which will probably have set up a "Victim's Assistance" office in the aftermath of violence. Talking to a professional gives you an opportunity to think out loud about strategies, as well as practice what you're going to say to your child.

2. **Express your concern to your child.** Gently say, "I love you and I'm concerned about you, and I want to make sure that you have every opportunity to get help in dealing with what happened." If the act of violence happened in your own community, you may want to say, "You, your friends, and their families have all gone through something terrible. But we're all going to get through this together. I promise you."

3. **Balance your child's day.** If necessary, lighten their stress and allow for activities that promote healing. This may mean a shortened school day. Discuss with their teachers reducing homework assignments. Cut back on stressful activities and engage them in fun, lighthearted activities.

4. Provide options for help and counseling. These might include:

- A family counselor who specializes in helping traumatized children

- A grief-support group at school

- A program at the local hospital, mental health center, outpatient clinic, or community center for kids who are traumatized.

- Reading materials and self-help websites that deal with grief and the aftermath of violence

COPING IN THE AFTERMATH

Support your child after a tragedy by showing patience and listening, not by providing easy answers or pressuring her to talk. The best thing you can do is just be there for your child. Resist the temptation to try to "fix" it for your child. No one can take away someone else's pain.

Relax. Seeing you "chill" will be a relief for your child, and open the door to exploring the "why?" questions together. It can also bring you closer to your child. Complicated feelings like survivor's guilt and the myriad other emotions that arise in grief require listening and reassurance on your part, not hurrying and lecturing.

In time, most children are going to be OK. For now, they are sad, scared, and confused. Commend them on their courage and what they are doing to help the injured, or honor a lost friend or classmate, or honor a child in another community.

If your child needs additional help, pursue the many resources for professional help in your community. Let him have a say in choosing the things that are going to help him heal. In these painful life lessons somehow we rise out of the ashes and manage to get through the toughest and saddest times. Your child will never be the same. But your child will be OK. Give it time.

HE AGES OF HIGHEST RISK FOR INITIATING SERIOUS VIOLENT BEHAVIOR ARE 15-16.—*YMCA*[1] ■ THE HIGHEST RATES

CHAPTER 10

N PARTICIPATION IN SERIOUS VIOLENCE ARE 16-17.—*YMCA*[1] ■ AFTER AGE 20, THE RISK OF INITIATING A PATTERN

OF VIOLENT BEHAVIOR IS CLOSE TO ZERO.—*NIH* ■ ARRESTS IN THE PAST DECADE JUMPED 63% FOR ROBBERY, 78%

WHAT'S

FOR AGGRAVATED ASSAULT AND 90% FOR MURDER.—*YWCA* ■ INTERVENTION PROGRAMS CAN BE COST-EFFECTIVE

BEING

AND CAN REDUCE THE LIKELIHOOD THAT YOUTHS WILL BECOME YOUTH OFFENDERS.—*USSG*[1] ■ YOUTH CRIME

DONE TO

AND VIOLENCE RATES COULD BE "SUBSTANTIALLY" REDUCED BY REALLOCATING MONEY TO MORE EFFECTIVE

CREATE

POLICIES AND PROGRAMS.—*USSG*[5] ■ EVALUATIONS OF POSITIVE YOUTH DEVELOPMENT PROGRAMS,

SAFE

LIKE THE BOYS AND GIRLS CLUBS AND THE BIG BROTHERS BIG SISTERS OF AMERICA PROGRAMS HAVE

SCHOOLS?

SHOWN REDUCTIONS IN VANDALISM, DRUG TRAFFICKING, AND YOUTH CRIME.—*USSG*[1] ■ BEHAVIORAL AND

SKILLS-ORIENTED STRATEGIES ARE AMONG THE MOST EFFECTIVE VIOLENCE PREVENTION APPROACHES. —*USSG*[1]

We have made great strides in our society in understanding the relationships between hatred and violence, bullying and violence, racism and violence, and television and violence. Most important, we have made it a priority to curb violence and prevent further tragedies. We still have a long way to go, however. Concerned parents, teachers, schools, community, and national organizations are working hard to prevent violence in our children's schools and communities, and they're starting to get results. This chapter describes the progress we've made so far.

SCHOOL SAFETY AND SECURITY PROGRAMS

In the wake of the recent tragedies in our nation, we have come to appreciate more than ever the protection and safety provided by our police, firefighters, and emergency workers. Although controversy exists about having police and security personnel patrolling on school campuses, there's little disagreement that they play a critical role in making our schools safer.

School safety and security programs combine preventive education, violence-prevention policies and practices, police presence, emergency response, and crisis intervention. Here are some important elements of these new programs:

- **Safety and security officers**—also called school resource officers—are a new breed of law enforcement that brings together the best aspects of school counselors and the police. Many such officers (called "narcs" by the kids in Southern California) formerly worked in the military, law enforcement, or juvenile justice. Their work is focused on education and violence prevention, but if a violent act or threat occurs, they know how to intervene and minimize the danger. The Santana High School safety and security officer is believed to have saved up to fifteen lives during the March 2001 shootings at that school.

- **Community police officers** work in and around schools and function as liaisons to the local police department. They purposely work out of offices in the community or school rather than at the precinct in order to be in a better position to detect threats of violence and quickly intervene.

- **Private security guards** are contracted by schools to patrol school campuses and enforce school safety policies.

- **Police substations** are set up either at schools or near them to provide high-risk areas with resources in a crisis.

- **Threat response and intervention programs** deal with threats and students issuing threats. These programs clearly define policies and procedures for how threats are reported, investigated and handled. Students learn they are expected to inform school authorities if they know about a threat. Parents learn that their child will be held accountable for making a threat of any kind. Parents of students who make threats are contacted and expected to provide information to help evaluate the seriousness of the threat.

- **Safety seminars and school assemblies** presented by experts in the field provide real power to kids and school personnel through knowledge and information. They give the real facts about threats of violence, teach prevention measures that students can use, and help identify areas where there is tension in the community.

- **800-number hotlines and tip lines** are now used in many schools. The hotline number is printed on every student's ID card. Students can call these toll-free numbers anonymously to report threats, assaults, suspected weapon possession by a classmate, or other safety concerns.

- **School safety design,** such as secure doors and windows (steel or bulletproof), having one main campus entrance, "maximum visibility" lighting and landscaping, and weapons detectors all contribute to making schools safe. Chain-link fences may not be attractive, but they keep out kids who don't belong on school grounds.

- **"Secure" technology,** such as video monitoring, alarm systems, emergency telephones, and student photo IDs are used in combination with improved safety design.

- **Federal violence-prevention programs** developed by the Department of Education and the Secret Service are available for presentation in your school district. Specialists explain to teachers, students, and school personnel how to prevent incidents of school violence through early detection. Lives have already been saved through these programs.

- **Safety laws** are being proposed and enacted in every state to prevent school violence. (*See Online Resource Directory.*)

ESTABLISH TIES TO THE POLICE

The time to get to know your local police department—particularly the officers assigned to your child's school—is before a crisis happens. Here are suggestions of how to accomplish this:

- **Pay a visit to your local police department** to see exactly what they do to prevent school violence and to ask how you can support them in their efforts.

- **Join a "ride-along" program** and learn to see your community as the police see it—through the windows of a patrol car.

- **Report trouble when you see it.** You and your child are the best eyes and ears the police have. Report potentially violent situations.

- **Share your concerns about police safety practices.** Occasionally, we read about a juvenile who is accidentally shot by an officer or becomes the unfortunate victim of a high-speed police chase and wonder if it could have been prevented. Constructively share your concerns with the community relations officer at your local police department and join the continual effort to improve upon police safety practices.

Police presence on campus is preventive. By being a part of the school community, police and safety personnel get to know the students as people, and students become more comfortable telling them about the problems, risks, and dangers in their school. Federal and state aid of more than $1 billion are now available for school-based partnerships with law enforcement agencies in safety programs. *(See Online Resource Directory.)*

BULLY-FREE SCHOOL BUS PROGRAMS

The school bus represents an unsupervised setting between home and school where kids of different ages come together every day—and where they are especially vulnerable to teasing, rough-housing, intimidation, and bullying. On their way to school, kids who are feeling anxious or upset can be susceptible to bullying—or to being bullies themselves. Coming home, when kids are decompressing, the same situations arise. On the school bus children are also more likely to bend to peer pressure since it can seem like a "no-win" situation on a moving vehicle. Clear bus-conduct policies should be established for students and drivers.

PREVENTION:

1. Present clear rules for bus behavior to all students and staff. Strict adherence to a school bus safety code sets a precedent for order and respect in the schoolroom.

2. Set up a session for drivers to learn the school's bus-conduct rules.

3. Arrange to have an assembly for students to get to know the bus drivers and talk about bus conduct. The goal is for students to attach a name and sense of authority to bus drivers so they will respect drivers and bus-conduct rules. Many schools report that hosting a bus driver appreciation day has provided the first step for students to go to bus drivers for help when they need it.

INTERVENTION:

1. Set up a warning system. Students should know that disciplinary measures will be taken when they break bus-conduct rules.

2. Suspend kids from riding the bus if they repeatedly misbehave—consider a "three strikes and you're out" system.

3. When certain situations violate the conduct code, authorize the driver to stop the school bus and separate the students involved in the conflict. For example, the driver might seat one child in the first row, and the other in the last.

SCHOOL ACTIVITIES THAT KEEP KIDS SAFE

- **School counselors** have saved countless lives and prevented untold incidents by staging interventions with potentially violent children.

- **Peer counseling programs** are made up of kids age sixteen and older who have been trained to help other kids with problems ranging from poor grades to drug and alcohol abuse. Peer counselors are often the only link that kids who feel isolated and desperate have to someone their own age. A peer understands firsthand the pressures and problems of being a teenager. One talk with a peer counselor may diffuse the anger building up inside a troubled child. Find out if there is peer counseling in your child's school.

- **Mediation programs** have proven effective at stemming potentially violent situations on high school campuses. Mediators—who can be peer or adult counselors—act as go-betweens, facilitating dialogue between feuding individuals and groups.

- **Violence-prevention classes, clubs, and assemblies** are often part of today's school curriculum. These classes teach nonviolent conflict resolution—how to diffuse racial tension, anti-bullying techniques, anger management, and effective communications skills. Some elementary schools have had tremendous success incorporating violence-prevention lessons and exercises into daily homeroom sessions. School assemblies featuring students speaking to the entire school about personal experiences with bullying, harassment, or threats have made long-lasting impressions on peers.

- **Anger management classes** help kids learn what triggers anger, how to handle being upset, and how to stand up for themselves—without anyone getting hurt. Kids also learn simple calming, "centering" and cooling off techniques. They gain insight into what happens emotionally when their "buttons" are pushed. For example, "Whatever name I'm being called isn't about me. So I have no reason to feel as though I have to defend myself."

■ **Organized sports,** from soccer to skateboarding, provide healthy outlets for aggression. Sportsmanship builds character and teaches kids to compete without losing control. Athletes learn to respect their adversaries and come to terms with winning and losing. Most communities offer organized sports for every level of skill. Even if your child isn't the best athlete, encourage him to participate at the appropriate skill level. Your child can have the same positive experiences regardless of his age or ability.

■ **The arts**—acting, playing a musical instrument, singing, dancing, painting and drawing—introduce children to the elements of cooperation, challenge, and patience. Kids find a healthy outlet for their emotions, plus they develop skills and expertise they can be proud of. Some art programs make violence their focus, with original plays and music that teach prevention. Teachers use creative techniques like role-playing, art, and poster making to dramatize nonviolence. *(See Online Resource Directory for examples.)*

AFTER-SCHOOL PROGRAMS

Kids who are unsupervised and running the streets often turn to violence to resolve differences. Where in our communities can our children go after school to learn new skills, get along with other kids, and have fun? Where do they go to turn their boredom into curiosity, try new sports or hobbies, learn from mentors, and stay out of trouble? Children who find it difficult to "fit in" in school sometimes discover that supervised after-school activities offer greater acceptance and provide much needed self-esteem. In addition to the many outstanding YMCAs and Boys and Girls Clubs, there are plenty of other terrific after-school programs:

■ **After-school clubs** are part of the extracurricular programs of most schools. In addition to athletics and intramural sports, there are activity-oriented clubs for an array of hobbys and study pursuits. Many schools sponsor local chapters of national organizations such as 4-H and SAVE (Students Against Violence Everywhere). Encourage your child to obtain their school's roster of clubs and join one which appeals to their interests. Only suggest additional activities if you feel your child can handle it. Offer your help and plan this together.

- **Martial arts, gymnastics, and yoga classes** offer kids a healthy outlet for expressing themselves. They not only become fit but build their self-confidence. If your child's school doesn't offer these kinds of activities, ask their athletic director or health and wellness teacher for recommendations. Many of these places offer free or single-class try-outs at reduced cost. Encourage your child to try one or more of these and then enroll in the class they like best.

- **Church and youth programs** make a huge difference in many kids' lives, both physically and spiritually. If your church or synagogue doesn't have a youth program, maybe others do, perhaps even a church of another denomination.

- **Parks and police departments** usually offer sports or other after-school activities. Call your police department to get information about the Police Athletic League (PAL) or your parks department to find out about other youth programs.

- **Community organizations and youth centers** frequently offer programs to engage kids in positive activities in the after-school hours.

- **Outdoor education and adventure programs** teach kids responsibility, cooperation and survival skills. Groups of kids under adult supervision go into the wilderness and learn to fend for themselves. Children get outstanding opportunities to work together as a team, commune with nature, get along with others and build confidence.

> *Reality Check* If you want to find out who offers programs of interest to your child, don't be afraid to try it! Calling strangers and being shuffled from person to person in a quest for information can be frustrating and discouraging. But more than ever before, people want to help. First write down a list of questions. Then, call local organizations, local businesses and your child's school. The process will become easier and in time, your child will follow your example.

NATIONAL PROGRAMS

National organizations like the Children's Defense Fund (CDF) and Educators for Social Responsibility (ESR) focus on ensuring healthy development for all children. Both organizations have set the standard for violence prevention by promoting educational reform and providing information, statistics, research, and model programs. These efforts help children develop emotionally and socially to reduce aggressive behavior and intolerance. They also help schools create safe learning environments that are prepared for any crisis.

In a sense, national organizations serve as role models for statewide and community organizations. Grassroots organizations can look to national organizations' methodologies to aid in all stages of development, from planning through program implementation and beyond. Similarly, local organizations can learn from national organizations what has worked and what hasn't.

COMMUNITY PROGRAMS

An example of a grassroots success story, Community Peacemakers of Oakland, California is a community-based violence prevention program which brings together schools, media, business, government, law enforcement, faith-based organizations, and social services. Community Peacemaker's "Kids are Street Safe Campaign" joins these separate entities in a collective effort to improve the quality of life, safety, and health of all children. This program is now nationally sponsored by the "Street Safe Kids" program. Both operate as the mainstay programs of its founding organization to offer tools, resources, and training in the Bay Area and across the country.

When Not to Keep a Secret, another grassroots organization, successfully shows children how to report weapons on campus without endangering themselves. Children learn that they can't remain silent or hope someone else will take care of the problem.

As more local and national organizations get involved to help kids stay safe, the need for cooperation and coordination is even greater. Contact one of the violence prevention programs available in your community and get involved. Many organizations are listed in the Online Resource Directory.

"AT-RISK" KIDS: WHO THEY ARE AND HOW WE CAN HELP THEM

At-risk kids—whether our own or someone else's—are often the ones who fall through the cracks in our society. They are kids who, for whatever reason, face difficult challenges in learning and fitting in. It's common sense that children who are "at-risk" must be identified early and given the help they need. Without help, their anger and frustration can escalate into violent, antisocial behavior.

At-risk kids include those who have the potential for violence and their potential victims, such as a child who is being bullied and may strike back.

8 WARNING SIGNS OF A POTENTIALLY VIOLENT CHILD

1. **Doesn't get along with other children.** Frequent fights and arguments with other children are signs a child needs help.

2. **Suffers from depression.** Major depression can be a precursor to violent behavior and needs to be treated professionally.

3. **Is too easily influenced.** Kids who are desperate for acceptance and status will often follow others into danger.

4. **Strongly opposes authority.** Resists, rebels, and defies authority; sees himself as a "victim" and has a "chip on his shoulder."

5. **Lays blame everywhere else.** Denies any responsibility for problems—it's always someone else's fault.

6. **Throws fits and tantrums.** Has repressed anger, which may not be seen until it builds into an explosion.

7. **History of violent behavior.** Has become violent, hurt animals, started fires in the past—and shown little remorse.

8. **Is failing in school.** Poor adjustment to school, lateness, truancy, frequent suspensions, falls further and further behind and has no motivation.

See the Online Resource Directory for a list of more indicators of at-risk behavior.

HOW TO HELP YOUR AT-RISK CHILD

Not surprisingly, our courts, youth camps, and jails are overflowing with at-risk children. Their parents are discouraged, overwhelmed, and most of them are desperately trying to save their children's lives. Here are suggestions to help at-risk kids:

1. **Keep them productively busy.** The last thing at-risk kids need is time on their hands. Most incidents of juvenile violence, accidents, and crimes occur after school. This is why after-school programs are so essential, especially in high-crime, violence-prone areas.

2. **Meet with your child's teachers regularly.** If your child is at-risk, stay in close touch with his school. Talk to his teachers, school counselor, and adults who have contact with him on a daily basis. Catch problems early and build on even the slightest progress.

3. **Ask for an educational or behavioral assessment.** When requested, most schools are required to test and evaluate your child. Discuss the results and recommendations with the principal, school counselor, and/or a child specialist. Then, follow up. Make sure the recommendations don't get lost in a filing cabinet.

4. **Become better informed about programs for at-risk kids.** Look into special programs at your child's school and in your community. Sit in on a class and afterward discuss your child's needs with the teacher or program director.

HELP PREVENT VIOLENCE IN ANOTHER CHILD

If you learn of a child who is violent or posing a serious threat, proceed cautiously. If there's time, you'll want to talk to other concerned witnesses and document the problem. Then, make the school principal and/or the child's family aware of your concerns. If you fail to get a satisfactory response and the problem persists, contact the police or a youth violence-prevention agency as your next step.

By reaching out to all at-risk children through their school, youth services, and mentoring programs, we make the streets and schools safer for everybody.

10 WAYS CHILDREN CAN MAKE SAFER SCHOOLS

Our kids play an active part in making their schools safer. Their choices to respect others, help solve mutual problems, and reduce tensions are important contributions to preventing violence and promoting safety. Plus, they are a living example to younger students. To keep their school safe, kids can:

1. **Organize a violence-prevention program**—a workshop, forum, or discussion group at their school, church, synagogue, or community center. This kind of initiative benefits the community and helps children develop leadership, organizational, and brainstorming skills.

2. **Train and serve as a peer mediator.** Children involved with peer mediation help their fellow students feel understood. Simultaneously their own interpersonal and problem-solving skills are strengthened. This instills self-confidence in the peer mediator and the child they're helping.

3. **Give the antiviolence issue a voice.** Circulate violence-free and drug-free pledges. Write articles or editorials in the school or community newspaper advocating for safer schools.

4. **Report weapons possession, threats, bullying, vandalism, or drug activity.** Encourage your child to value herself and others by taking action in the name of safety.

5. **Participate in school or community programs** to help make their school and neighborhood safer.

6. **Volunteer as a mentor, Big Brother, or Big Sister** to an at-risk kid.

7. **Participate with fellow students** in violence-prevention initiatives, including conflict-resolution programs and classes, and school assemblies.

8. **Write or call television stations, movie studios, and video game makers** asking them to reduce the level of violence in their programming.

9. **Boycott movies, television shows, toys, and video games that are excessively violent.** Take a stand. Write to companies that make these products for kids and tell them that you are boycotting them. Tell the media, too. Send a message.

10. **Urge peers not to experiment with drugs and alcohol.** When urging isn't enough, get help. Walk them to a drug counselor, an AA meeting, or into a drug or alcohol rehabilitation program. Don't wait until their drinking or drug use becomes a problem. Be a real friend and say something.

Safer communities are built one person at a time.

AFTERWORD: COPING IN OUR VIOLENT WORLD

O nly a few years ago, school shootings were inconceivable. Sadly, "Columbine" is now rooted in our collective memory. Since the September 11, 2001, terrorist attacks, we have been placed on "high alert." All of us, to some degree, feel vulnerable and defenseless. Many of our children feel uneasy in their schools; many parents feel uneasy most of the time. As individuals and as a nation we never had to deal with these kinds of threats. We're all worried, and we all try to cope with our growing anxiety.

What is the healthy way to cope in our violent world? We first must recognize that we cannot be in control of everything. There are students who pick up weapons and use violence to settle scores. There are people "out there" who have no regard for human life and would participate in another terrorist attack. Though we realize it may not be possible to completely protect ourselves, we must strive to make intelligent choices and take precautions that will maximize our chances of survival. We support and count on the police and firefighters in our communities and, on a federal level, the military and our government leaders to protect us. Most important, we take personal responsibility—for ourselves and for our children.

To cope with the threats of violence in our children's world we have to instill safety, not fear, in our children. It is of paramount importance in these troubling times that you stay available to them in an ongoing, vital sense:

- Talk about how you feel—vent your own fears and anxieties and discuss them as a family.

- Assure your kids about all the things that are being done to ensure their safety, and be sure it is!

- Maintain routines. Keeping the flow of family life on an even keel allays our own anxiety as well as theirs.

- Convert your anxiety into actions that will help you stay calm: write in a journal, draw or paint to express your fears; take a trip or a walk and connect with nature.

- Schedule "quiet time" not just for your kids but for yourself to ease stress.

- Stay in touch with extended family and friends. Plan get-togethers to affirm your sense of connection to community.

- Engage in activities like prayer and community gatherings that allow you to hope for the best and work for peace.

- Get professional help if necessary to learn new coping skills or reenergize your old ones.

- Above all, stay strong. We cannot allow ourselves to be seduced into extreme fear or denial.

We're doing a lot. But there is still so much more we can do. Our kids are one of life's greatest gifts, and parenting is one of life's greatest challenges. Our greatest joy derives from our children, so when bad things happen to them, there is no greater sorrow. Talking to your children about how to keep themselves safe and our world safe may not always be easy, but it's the best investment you can make in their happiness and well-being.

Reality Check Reading a "How-to" book about parenting can be inspiring—and overwhelming. There's so much to do, so much to remember. We don't quite know how we're going to put everything we learned into action. Or whether we'll do it right. My advice is to slow down and take a deep breath. Good parenting happens a lesson at a time. Do the best you can. And pat yourself on the back for trying to become an even better mom or dad. God bless you and your family. And safe passage.

ABOUT THE AUTHORS

Ken Druck, Ph.D., is the executive director of the Jenna Druck Foundation, which he founded in 1996 following the tragic death of his daughter. The Foundation's two nonprofit programs, Families Helping Families and Young Women's Leadership, assist families after the death of a child and develop critical skills in young women leaders. Dr. Druck is often called upon to help families and schools in crisis such as Columbine and Santana High School after the shootings in those communities. Since September 11, 2001, he has been assisting families in New York, through the New York Fire Department and World Trade Center Family Counseling Center, as well as in California.

Dr. Druck is also a consulting psychologist, executive coach, team-building specialist, speaker and best-selling author. After more than 20 years in clinical practice with leaders in business and government, he began Druck Enterprises, Inc. His broad base of clients has included Microsoft, IBM, Pharmacia, Sempra Energy, Mirage Resorts, Jewel, YMCA, and the San Diego Unified School District. His corporate programs, geared to executives and their teams, teach integrity, resilience, high-level communication, and teamwork.

Ken Druck's innovative work has been featured on Oprah, CNN, ABC, HBO, and PBS specials, as well as in major newspapers and magazines including *The New York Times, L.A. Times, Chicago Tribune, USA Today, Nation's Business, Parade,* and *U.S. News and World Report.* He is the author of *The Secrets Men Keep* and writes regularly for *Family Circle* magazine.

Early in his career, Dr. Druck worked with inner city teens in New York City and as a psychologist with Spanish Peaks Community Mental Health Center in Colorado. Throughout the years, he has been a strong advocate for violence prevention, parent effectiveness and educational programs sensitive to the needs of children with learning differences.

Dr. Druck received his doctorate in clinical psychology from the Fielding Institute.

Matthew Kaplowitz has been involved with popular media for more than two decades as an Emmy®, Grammy®, and Peabody® award-winning producer and composer. His words and music are heard in innumerable programs for NBC, CBS, HBO, PBS, Sony, Disney Nickelodeon, and MTV, and in multimedia publications from Scholastic, Oxford University Press, and the American Foundation for the Blind. He was awarded honorary lifetime membership in the PTA in recognition of his volunteer work with learning-disabled children.

Ken Blanchard, Ph.D., is chief spiritual officer of The Ken Blanchard Companies, the San Diego-based international management training and consulting firm, founded in 1979, that lists among its clients General Motors, IBM, and Amway. He is the author of the phenomenal bestseller, *The One Minute Manager*, and several successive volumes, including the just-published *The One Minute Apology*. His book on spirituality in the workplace, *Leadership by the Book*, has given new meaning to Servant Leadership. Dr. Blanchard's many awards and honors for his contributions in the field of management leadership include the Council of Peers Award of Excellence from the National Speakers Association and the Golden Gavel Award from Toastmasters International. He is cofounder of the Center for FaithWalk Leadership, which is dedicated to helping leaders walk their talk in the marketplace.

Arnie Levin has been a contract artist for *The New Yorker* for almost thirty years, producing over 700 cartoons and 27 covers. He has illustrated and contributed to many books, including *The Money Book for Kids*, *The Enormous Baby*, *The Smile Book*, *Free to Be a Family*, and *Homer and the House Next Door*, and in addition has created numerous short films for Sesame Street and The Electric Company.

He has twice received the Magazine Cartoonist of the Year Award from the National Cartoonist Society.

ACKNOWLEDGMENTS

The editorial genius, sensibility and dedication of Matt Kaplowitz have guided this book from its inception. I am sustained by the abiding love and support of family and friends, especially Diane Roberts, Joelle James, Karen Druck, Roberta and Scott Pirrello, Asa Baber, "the Goonies," Irv Schuster, Helen "Wheels" Robbins, and my family at the Jenna Druck Foundation. Special thanks to Natasha Padilla and the gang at "Ono" for their huge contribution. Gratitude always to Roslyn and Charles, my parents.   —K.D.

My deep appreciation and admiration to Erin Clermont, editor, for her superb editorial insight and guidance, to Raymond Hooper, for his brilliant design and tireless efforts, and to Mike Lovett for his support and encouragement from the very beginning.   —M.K.

STATISTICS ABBREVIATION KEY

ABBREVIATIONS/CITATIONS:

AACAP   American Academy of Child and Adolescent Psychiatry

AAP   American Academy of Pediatrics

ABC   March 7, 2000, ABCNews.com. (from Maryland State Commission on Criminal Sentencing Policy: http://www.msccsp.org/resources/juvenile.html)

AMA   American Medical Association (from PREVENTING SCHOOL VIOLENCE. Prepared Exclusively for the California State Senate, Committee on Education, Written by Michele Borba, Ed.D)

APA   American Psychological Association (from PREVENTING SCHOOL VIOLENCE. Prepared Exclusively for the California State Senate, Committee on Education, Written by Michele Borba, Ed.D)

BORBA[1]   PREVENTING SCHOOL VIOLENCE. Prepared Exclusively for the California State Senate, Committee on Education, Written by Michele Borba, Ed.D.

BORBA[2]   PREVENTING SCHOOL VIOLENCE. Prepared Exclusively for the California State Senate, Committee on Education, Written by Michele Borba, Ed.D. (Fields, G.,& Overberg, P. 1998, March 26. "Juvenile Homicide Arrest Rate on Rise in Rural USA." USA Today, sec. A, p. 11)

CDC[1]   Centers for Disease Control & Prevention: *School Killings Found to Have Yearly Pattern*, 2001.

CDC[2]   Centers for Disease Control & Prevention, 1998

CDF   Children's Defense Fund (http://www.childrensdefense.org/data.php)

CRA   Arnold Goldstein, Director of the Center for Research on Agression at Syracuse University; author, *Violence in America* p. 15

GCU   Garbarino, Cornell University.

FBI[1]   Federal Bureau of Investigation (from PREVENTING SCHOOL VIOLENCE. Prepared Exclusively for the California State Senate, Committee on Education, Written by Michele Borba, Ed.D)

FBI[2]   Federal Bureau of Investigation (from 1999 YWCA WEEK WITHOUT VIOLENCE toolkit)

FBI[3]   U.S. Department of Justice: Federal Bureau of Investigation, The School Shooter: *A Threat Assessment Perspective*, 1999. (http://www.usdoj.gov/youth violence.htm)

JAACAP   The Journal of the American Academy of Child and Adolescent Psychiatry, August 23, 2000 (HealthCentral.com) (from State Commission on Criminal Sentencing Policy: http://www.msccsp.org/resources/juvenile.html)

JIE   Josephson Institute of Ethics

NEA   National Education Association

NICHD   National Institute of Child Health and Human Development/Nansel

NIH   National Youth Survey—National Institute of Health. NIH Publication No. 01-4588 (http://www.nimh.nih.gov/publicat/teens.cfm)

NIMF   National Institute on Media and
        the Family

NFCCHM Nemours Foundation's Center for
        Children's Health Media Updated
        and reviewed by: Fred Fow, MD,
        Date reviewed: January 2002,
        Originally reviewed by: Paul
        Robins, PhD

NYGC   National Youth Gang Center:
        National Youth Gang Survey, 1999.

NYS/NIH National Youth Survey—National
        Institute of Health. NIH Publication
        No. 01-4588 (http://www.nimh.nih.
        gov/publicat/teens.cfm)

NYT/CBS New York Times/CBS News poll,
        Oct. 1999 (from PREVENTING
        SCHOOL VIOLENCE. Prepared
        Exclusively for the California State
        Senate, Committee on Education,
        Written by Michele Borba, Ed.D)

OKIE[1] *Washington Post,* Wednesday, April
        25, 2001; Page A08

OKIE[2] Washington Post, Wednesday, April
        25, 2001; Page A08 (National
        SAFE KIDS Campaign)

SDDA   San Diego District Attorney's office

US DOE[1] U.S. Department of Education, 1998.

US DOE[2] U.S. Department of Education,
        *Indicators of School Crime and
        Safety 2001.* (U.S. Department of
        Education, National Center for
        Education Statistics, Fast
        Response Survey System,
        "Principal/School Disciplinarian
        Survey on School Violence," FRSS
        63, 1997.)

US DOH   U.S. Department of Health

US DOJ   1996 Uniform Crime Report.
        Washington, DC: U.S. Department
        of Justice. (from PREVENTING
        SCHOOL VIOLENCE. Prepared
        Exclusively for the California State
        Senate, Committee on Education,
        Written by Michele Borba, Ed.D)

US N&WR U.S. News & World Report

USSG[1] U.S. Surgeon General, *Youth
        Violence: A Report of the Surgeon
        General*

USSG[2] U.S. Surgeon General, *Youth
        Violence: A Report of the Surgeon
        General,* (Dumas 1989)

USSG[3] U.S. Surgeon General, *Youth
        Violence: A Report of the Surgeon
        General,* (Loeber et al., 1998;
        Moffitt, 1993; Tolan, 1987; Tolan &
        Gorman-Smith, 1998)

USSG[4] U.S. Surgeon General, *Youth
        Violence: A Report of the Surgeon
        General,* (Bry, 1982; Bry & George,
        1979, 1980)

USSG[5] U.S. Surgeon General, *Youth
        Violence: A Report of the Surgeon
        General,* (Mendel, 2000, p. 1)

USSS   U.S. Secret Service

YWCA[1] 1999 YWCA WEEK WITHOUT
        VIOLENCE toolkit

ONLINE RESOURCE DIRECTORY

Throughout the book we have described violence prevention strategies, school safety programs, after-school activities, high-risk factors for violent behavior, parenting techniques, and more. The *How to Talk to Your Kids About School Violence* website expands on this information and suggests programs, tools, and organizations to help you realize a safe and healthy life for you and your child. Listing hundreds of resources, including individual descriptions and contact information, the online resource directory is accessible at **www.howtotalktoyourkids.com**. Although this directory is not an exhaustive list of available resources, the information listed includes what we consider to be most helpful. Please note that these resources are just suggestions. We do not guarantee the information or actions of those mentioned. Following is a list of categories included in the resource directory:

15 Indicators for Identifying Troubled Youth

Articles, Books and Searches

Bullying and Anti-bullying/ Bullyproofing programs

Communicating with Our Children

Community, After-School & Summer Programs/Activities

Contracts & Pledges

Crisis Intervention & Bereavement Organizations

Department of Education state-by-state & territory listings

Dewey Decimal reference information

Domestic Violence and Abuse

Drug & Substance Abuse

Filtering Sites

Funding Resources

Gangs

Guns

Homeland Security

Hotlines

Internet Safety

Juvenile Justice Agency Representative state-by-state & territory listings

Mental Health

National Crisis & Information Hotlines

PTA Office state-by-state & territory listings

"Pledge to be Violence-Free"

Religious-Sponsored Youth Activities & Organizations

School Safety & Violence Prevention

School Shootings

Selected Articles, Books, and Searches

Spiritual Awareness

Violence in the Media

INDEX

RC: Reality Check